ACCESSIBILITY:
the rural challenge

ACCESSIBILITY:
the rural challenge

Malcolm J. Moseley

METHUEN & CO LTD   LONDON

First published in 1979 by
Methuen & Co Ltd
11 New Fetter Lane, London EC4P 4EE
© *1979 Malcolm J. Moseley*

Typeset by Red Lion Setters, Holborn, London.
Printed in Great Britain at the
University Press, Cambridge

ISBN 0 416 71220 7 (hardbound)
ISBN 0 416 71230 4 (paperback)

To the memory of my mother

Contents

List of figures

Acknowledgements

Much of this book stems from the Rural Transport and Accessibility research project which I directed from 1975-7 at the University of East Anglia. The project was sponsored by the Department of the Environment and the final report was published in two volumes (Moselet *et al.*, 1977). I am grateful to the Department for their support, and also to my colleagues Oliver Coles, Reg Harman, Gwen Hughes and Mike Spencer who worked jointly on the project and who were directly and deeply involved in the collection and analysis of information upon which that final report, and indirectly this book, have been based. Peter Wilmers and Peter Jones made very useful comments on a draft, and I am grateful to them for the care with which they approached the task. Given that this book amounts to a personal and subsequent reflection upon that work and upon a mass of other evidence, then of course no-one but myself can in any way be held responsible for its contents.

I am also grateful to Gwen Hughes, Susan Winston and Pauline Blanch for diligently typing the various drafts, and to the Nuffield Foundation for a small grant to defray certain secretarial expenses. David Mew and Paul Crysell drew the majority of the diagrams, and Peter Scott photographed them.

The following authors and organizations kindly agreed to my reproducing figures from their publications: Dr Brian Woodruffe, Dr Paul Cloke, Professor R.J. Johnston, Mr John Madgett, Mrs Susan Owens, the Transport and Road Research Laboratory, Koninklijk Nederlands Aardrijkskundig Genootschap, the Scottish Postal Board, the Association of Transport Coordinating Officers, the Derbyshire and Cumbria County Planning Officers, the editor of *Regional Studies*, Oxford University Press, the Eastern Counties Omnibus Co. Ltd, the Department of Environment.

Malcolm J. Moseley *June 1978*

1
Introduction

Introductory chapters, though normally read first, are often written last and this is no exception. Its purpose is to provide some justification for and reflection upon what follows and to that end it is useful to attempt it retrospectively.

Largely written in late 1977 and early 1978, this book draws substantially upon the work of the Rural Transport and Accessability research project which was published as Moseley *et al.* (1977) and is frequently cited below as 'the UEA study'. In building upon that report, the book presents and appraises some of its principal research findings and policy recommendations in a form which should be more readily available and comprehensible to those concerned with the rural accessibility problem, whether as students, practitioners or interested laymen. But it also aims to synthesize significant pieces of work undertaken by other researchers — the mid-1970s have been extremely fruitful in this respect — and to appraise policy developments up to early 1978.

The central theme of the book is accessibility — a concept explored in some detail in chapter 4, but basically relating to people's ability to reach the things which are important to them. And if rural areas are in essence those parts of the country where people and activities are widely spaced, then it should come as no surprise to learn that problems of inaccessibility are particularly serious there. Indeed they are linked with a number of more visible ills such as the inadequacy of employment opportunities, selective depopulation and repopulation, the isolation and loneliness of certain vulnerable groups and the disproportionately high cost of providing services. These and other problems, and their links with the pervading issue of insufficient accessibility, are explored principally in chapters 2 and 3.

Accessibility is very unequally distributed in rural areas. Not only do places or villages differ considerably in this respect, but so, too, do individual people — and it is they who are the proper focus of concern. There is a long history of academic study of inequalities in income, wealth, education, housing, power, etc. (see for example Wedderburn, 1974) but concern for personal variations in accessibility in a physical sense is more recent and ill-developed. And yet deprivation in this sphere can be equally serious, and as difficult to eradicate. Indeed, often it correlates at the household and individual level with these other, more familiar, elements of social and economic deprivation, and as an element of multiple deprivation it takes on extra force and urgency.

The fact that accessibility deprivation can only be expressed in relative terms — relative, that is, to the levels of access enjoyed by others in society — does not reduce its painfulness for those who suffer, or the importance of reducing it. Expectations and aspirations have risen enormously in rural Britain in the post-war period as the mass media have increased their penetration and as formerly urban residents have moved in in larger numbers. Couple this with the steady decline that has occurred in rural public transport and in rural service provision and it is not surprising that those people who have missed out on the dramatic rise in mobility and accessibility that car availability confers, have a strong and justified sense of grievance.

The present author is, of course, not the first to draw attention to this and the early/mid-1970s have witnessed a spate of studies and of policy initiatives. But if accessibility, as a concept and a problem, spans the whole spectrum of rural life, then so, too, should the decision-making machinery erected by society to deal with it. Unfortunately, relevant policies in the 1970s have in contrast been narrowly focused, ill-coordinated and *ad hoc*. Chapter 5 explores in depth the all-important fragmentation of decision-making and public expenditure in this field.

Subsequent chapters review the range of policy options which, if implemented, might improve the levels of accessibility presently enjoyed by disadvantaged rural residents. Like the relevant problems and decision-making agencies, these policy options are numerous, wide-ranging and rarely considered as a single package.

Logically there are four ways of overcoming the distance which separates carless rural residents and the services or activities to which they require access. The residents might be rendered more mobile by means of a variety of transport measures; alternatively the services themselves could be literally mobilized and taken out to the rural inhabitants. The second pair of options relates to land-use planning policy: rural residents might be gradually persuaded to live closer to the centres of service provision; or small 'outlets' of rural services could be maintained or provided in the remoter areas. Each of these areas of policy subsumes a large number of more precise policy options, and we are led to consider, for instance, rural bus subsidies, playbuses, rural council housing and village school closures — to take just one example from each area. None of these policy areas provides a panacea, but none can be ignored.

The final chapter outlines some directions which policy could usefully take. It relates both to the individual policy elements previously reviewed and to the *process* whereby those elements should be considered and, if appropriate, implemented. Improved coordination is seen to be of paramount importance — not just in terms of the knitting together of public transport timetables and routes, but in the more fundamental sense of bringing together a mass of largely autonomous public agencies into a common decision-making framework. The planning process, incorporating explicit attempts to derive and weight objectives and to formulate and evaluate alternative policies in the light of those objectives, needs to become the accepted procedure for reaching accessibility-related decisions. And it must be the county councils who develop this accessibility planning function and who bring together the other agencies under a common umbrella.

None of this, however, can be achieved without adequate political will. This book merely outlines *why* the rural accessibility problem is serious and *how* it might best be attacked. But *whether* the necessary reforms and initiatives will actually be undertaken depends in large part upon the attitudes and priorities of central and local government politicians, and upon their willingness and ability to redirect the efforts of the public and private sectors. This theme is latent in the various chapters of the book.

But to spell out its significance a little more clearly, two very recent and different pieces of evidence may be cited. Analysis of the expenditure on transport which has been planned by non-metropolitan county councils and accepted by the Department of Transport as a basis for Transport Supplementary Grant payments for the year 1978-9 (a major channel for rural transport financing, discussed in chapter 5) reveals that of a total of £356 million only £30 million (8.4 per cent) is destined for the revenue support of public transport. In some counties this figure falls as low as 3 per cent (Oxfordshire) or 4 per cent (Suffolk) while for the principal *urban* areas (the Greater London Council and the metropolitan counties taken together) it is 22 per cent (British Road Federation, 1977). Yet it is *this* area of transport expenditure, rather than the construction and maintenance of roads and car parks, which directly benefits those who lack cars in rural areas.

Doubtless in part these disparities reflect differing local circumstances, but in part they surely also stem from deep-seated ideological differences. Though there are important exceptions, the local councils responsible for service provision in rural areas typically pursue low rate, low expenditure, policies. Public transport, public housing and similar public services tend to attract less political support there than in the conurbations. Indeed, an important conclusion of Rose's recent (1978) and detailed study of local government in Suffolk is that often 'there is a deeply entrenched view that politics should not enter local government. The job of the councillor is to pursue the public interest, and the public interest is not seen as problematic but obvious.' He argues that 'the consequences of "keeping politics out of local government" are that the powerful not only continue to govern in their own interests, but do so unopposed.'

This is a contentious conclusion and whether it is true of other parts of rural Britain is open to debate, but it is clear that questions of values, attitudes and the distribution of power in rural society, though not explored in any depth in this book, rarely lies far beneath the surface of the rural accessibility problem. How far society gets to grips with the problems and opportunities which are explored below will depend in large part upon this socio-political dimension. But in so far as these problems and opportunities are imperfectly understood at present, then this book may serve a useful purpose.

2
Rural Britain
in transition

There is no unambiguous way of defining 'rural areas'. Their perceived extent will vary according to whether attention is directed to economic criteria (e.g., high dependence upon agriculture), social and demographic criteria (e.g., the 'rural way of life' or low population density) or geographical criteria (e.g., remoteness from urban centres). But obviously a good deal of common ground is to be found. A Department of Environment study carried out in 1971 mapped rural areas on the basis of just three factors — population density, the proportion of resident males employed in agriculture and related occupations, and the degree of dependence upon other local authority areas for employment purposes (Countryside Review Committee, 1977). More recently, Cloke (1977) has synthesized a whole range of apparently relevant indices to produce a single 'index of rurality' (figure 2.1). What is clear is that there are peaks, troughs and gradations of rurality; not clear breakpoints.

It is more useful to stress the variety of rural areas, and the importance of their interaction with the towns where most British people live and work. Two basic sorts of rural area may in fact be distinguished. Those remote from the main urban areas tend to display a declining, static or only very modestly increasing population; a declining number of working males; an ageing population structure often with low rates of natural increase; declining employment; low female activity rates; and a high per capita cost of service provision. On the other hand, the 'dormitory or exurban areas', within commuting distance of the major conurbations or other large towns, tend to show a rapid increase in population; a high proportion of workers travelling out of the area to work each day; a youthful population structure; and particularly high levels of car ownership. The characteristics of rural areas, then, vary, but all are inextricably linked with urban Britain by migration flows — whether of the young, the economically active or the retired — and by the linkage effected by commuting, recreational activity, the movement of raw

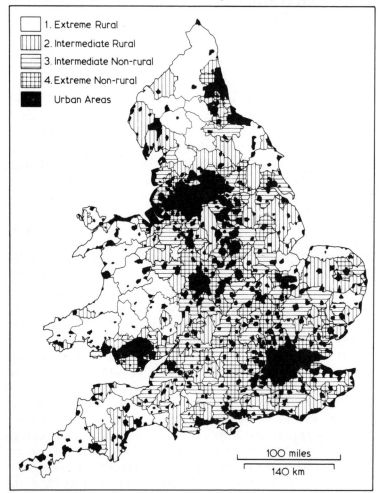

1. Extreme Rural
2. Intermediate Rural
3. Intermediate Non-rural
4. Extreme Non-rural
Urban Areas

100 miles
140 km

Figure 2.1 England and Wales: rurality in 1971
Source: Cloke (1977)

materials, agricultural produce and manufactured goods, and the expenditure of public and private sector resources.

The crucial characteristic of rural Britain which will be explored in this chapter is that of *change*. The society, economy and spatial structure of rural Britain are each changing rapidly, and it is within this context of change that both the rural accessibility problem and the range of possibly relevant policies must be understood.

The basic notion of accessibility has already been introduced; it embraces three components:

(i) people, the residents of rural areas;
(ii) the activities or services which they require;
(iii) the transport or communications link between the two.

The forces affecting the changing nature and location of each of these three basic components of rural accessibility must be explored. While it is not argued that change alone, whether viewed as the decline of rural bus services or of the village shop or whatever, constitutes the *only* justification for public intervention, it does tend to sharpen certain problems that are deep-seated and to add extra urgency to the call for action. And, as change occurs, certain policy options become untenable or redundant while others come to the fore.

One further, and perhaps obvious, introductory point: the elements of change are inextricably interlinked. One impetus for change — for example a personal decision to migrate from a rural village — will set in train a series of consequences. The village shopkeeper may move nearer bankruptcy, the bus service may become slightly less viable and, depending on who buys the vacated house, a new set of demands for public and private services will result. It is impossible to place into separate compartments what may be termed 'forces for change' and the 'responses to change', though much of chapter 3, with its concern for the casualties of change, seeks to focus on the latter.

Let us now take in some detail each of the three basic components of rural accessibility (people, activities and links), establish how they have been changing and speculate on their future development.

People

Both the size and the composition of the rural population affect the rural accessibility issue in two ways. First, they determine the scale of the demand or the need for private or public services. Second, they affect the 'supply' of accessibility by impinging on the viability of public transport, the availability of public-spirited volunteers, etc.

1 NUMBERS

Concerning the size of Britain's rural population, the first need is to dispel the myth that depopulation is the norm. Taking together the rural districts of England and Wales and the county districts of Scotland, their combined population was:

	million inhabitants	as % of national total
1951:	9.7	18.7%
1961:	10.4	19.4%
1971:	12.1	21.7%

Admittedly these old administrative rural districts contained large portions of suburbia but it is clear that for lowland England, at least, population growth has been the norm in the post-war period. Woodruffe's (1976) analysis of population change in 1951-61 and 1961-71 shows clearly that south and east of the 'Tees-Exe line', which crudely separates highland from lowland Britain, few areas experienced population decline in 1961-71 (only those which are stippled on his map, figures 2.2a and b). What has happened is that remoter, upland, Britain has frequently suffered a net decline in population because of potent economic forces, but that lowland England has largely offset this potential decline by the in-movement of retired or near-retired people and of economically active households with at least one member prepared to commute daily to an urban workplace.

Speculation about the future size of the rural population must take account of the marked decline in the national population growth rate which has occurred in the mid-late 1970s. But the migration by formerly urban residents into rural areas seems likely to continue — both in search of retirement and second homes and as a basis for commuting — even if house-price differentials narrow, and transport costs rise in real terms. Such migration probably reflects the fundamental life-style preferences regarding environment and space that many people hold. Two important things follow from this. First, there will remain a substantial rural population many of whom will have problems of access; second, by the end of the century a larger proportion of rural residents will live there by choice and not by dint of their place of birth or their employment.

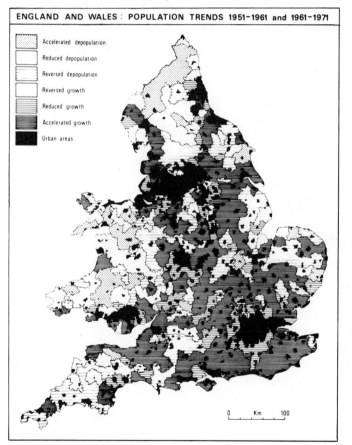

Figure 2.2a England and Wales: population trends 1951-61 and 1961-71
Source: Woodruffe (1976)

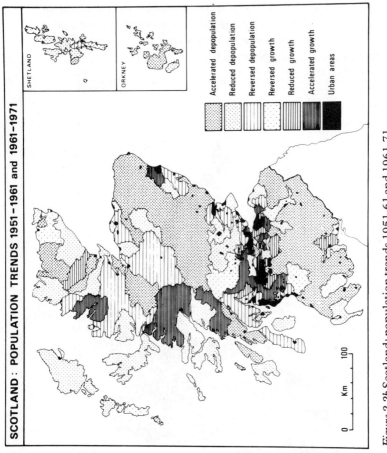

Figure 2.2b Scotland: population trends 1951-61 and 1961-71
Source: Woodruffe (1976)

2 COMPOSITION

So much for numbers. What of the changing composition of the
rural population? Two trends need to be stressed. The first is the
ageing process which is the product both of selective out-migration
which predominantly affects young adults and thereby the local
birth rate, and of selective in-migration, with retired people being
able to ignore the predominantly urban location of employment
opportunities. Many rural areas now have 20-30 per cent of their
population over the normal retirement age of 60 years (female)
and 65 years (male). (The national figure is 17 per cent.) All the
indications are that the contribution of the retired to the rural population structure will increase, particularly, of course, if the retirement age is reduced. A major attraction factor is the ability to make a
substantial capital gain from selling an urban or suburban pro-
perty, and as owner-occupation levels increase this may affect many
more elderly people. A corollary of all this is that in many rural areas
the school-age population will fall — even more substantially
than it will do nationally on account of the recent low birth rate.

The second social trend that must be mentioned because of its
relevance to accessibility is the increased heterogeneity of the rural
population. We must beware of speaking of rural 'communities' as
if they are coterminous with physical units such as rural 'villages'
(Martin, 1976). Often it is more accurate to recognize several
communities occupying the same physical space. Long-established
residents, oriented to the village and often doing manual work, live
in a different world from the middle-class newcomers who tend to
work, shop and establish social contacts in quite different areas. In
many villages at least three relatively separate communities may be
found — occupying the old settlement, the new council estate and
the new private residential estate.

3 VALUES AND ASPIRATIONS

It is probable that the post-war rise in what people expect or feel
entitled to in the way of public sector service provision in rural
areas is greater than the actual decline in that provision. In other
words, the widening gap between expectations and provision in
rural areas may well owe more to changes in the former. But rising

expectations are only one important relevant change: parallel to it has been a growing concern to be involved in or at least consulted in the decision-making which affects the quality of rural accessibility, and a concern also for greater equality of opportunity between urban and rural residents and between the different income groups. The key social contrasts today are not urban/rural but modern/traditional. As a result of migration, education and the universal penetration of the mass media, many rural people tend now to have what was previously seen as 'urban' aspirations. This poses serious difficulties for the various public authorities when it comes to determining the pattern of public expenditure.

4 LOCATION

Finally, what change in the distribution of population *within* rural areas has occurred in the post-war period and is likely to occur in the future? The main feature is that population growth has tended to correlate positively with proximity to the larger urban centres and with the size of the settlement itself. The smaller and the more remote settlements have tended to have a static or declining population. Equally important for the accessibility issue they have tended to have a markedly ageing population structure. Is this general tendency, reinforced in general by planning policy, of the increased concentration *within* rural areas of its economically active members likely to continue or be stemmed? This is an important question since it clearly has a direct effect upon the economic viability of public and private services. Developments in sewerage technology and in the harnessing of solar energy suggest that in the long run individual rural households may be able to be less dependent upon publicly provided services. Similarly, advances in telecommunications will permit a few — a select few — to work from home. But many services, e.g., water supply and school education, will continue to be provided from or at a central location, with population dispersal continuing to impose a clear cost on the community. Such dispersal seems unlikely to occur on a large scale, partly because of these community costs and partly because of the growing force of environmental pressure groups which are likely to continue to resist the dispersal of new development on landscape and amenity grounds.

Activities or services

One persistent trend has characterized the provision of services in post-war rural Britain — a tendency for service outlets to become fewer, larger and more widely spaced. Partly this reflects the scale economies enjoyed by many services — other things being equal it is cheaper to educate 100 children in one school than 25 in each of four schools — but it derives also from the substantial rise in mobility that car ownership has brought to the majority of households. The classic pattern of shopping for example, with daily, weekly and occasional shopping being directed to the village, small town and large town respectively, has been eroded by the 'multi-purpose trip' — the tendency for the motorist to bypass the village and small town shop for the greater range and convenience of large town shopping.

Considering *shopping* in some detail, the decline in village food shops in recent years has been quite marked. A survey of a sector in rural Norfolk stretching from Norwich to the coast revealed a reduction in the number of village shops in the period 1950-66 from 132 to 76 (Norfolk County Council, 1977). Nationally, the total number of shops fell from 583,000 in 1950 to 485,000 in 1971. No precise threshold, or minimum population size needed to support a village shop, can be defined but it is clear that villages with fewer than 250 residents have had most difficulty in keeping their shop. In 1976, as part of the UEA study, a survey was undertaken of 40 parishes in Norfolk with fewer than 800 inhabitants. Between them they mustered 43 shops:

65 per cent of the parishes has at least one shop;
75 per cent of the parishes had a post office (usually combined with the shop);
only 38 per cent of the parishes had a public house.

A survey of the proprietors of these village shops revealed two factors which bode ill for their future. First, the age of the proprietors: 70 per cent were over 45 years of age, and 25 per cent over 60 years. Many doubted whether the shop would continue in business on their retirement. Second, their reliance on the poorer members of their village, with the wealthier, more mobile residents making only infrequent purchases there. Another survey by the same research team, this time of the residents of many of the 40 parishes, confirmed this. Only 53 per cent of the respondents said that they used their local shop frequently. The main reasons for not using it were given as: prices too high; need to travel elsewhere anyway so shop there; limited stock, choice or range of commodities.

Probably many village retailers will remain in business for some years to come. Many have benefited from marketing adaptations — from joining SPAR or MACE type enterprises which enjoy the advantages of bulk buying and large-scale promotional services. Others see village retailing more as a way of life than as an exercise in profit maximization, and they work long hours for very little financial reward out of a feeling of responsibility to the community and a desire to remain part of that community. But a clear trend of decline is apparent.

The recent history of the dispensing chemist illustrates this well. Considering the smaller chemist (those dispensing fewer than 12,000 prescriptions per year) these comprised 43 per cent of the total in 1961 but only 16 per cent in 1972. A recent report in *The Times* (4 August 1977) revealed that 300 chemists' shops are closing each year, and that a third of Britain's 9600 chemists are losing about £1000 per year. Most of these, of course, are in the urban areas, but the implications for rural residents, especially those without a car, seem serious.

Taking *employment* as an 'activity' to which rural residents require access, the most significant rural trend has of course been the marked decline in the number of agricultural jobs available. Over the past 25 years the average annual rise in labour productivity in agriculture has been around 6 per cent, as the industry has become mechanized and modernized and as farms have been amalgamated. The workforce has fallen by 2-3 per cent per annum, so that today less than 3 per cent of the British workforce is in agriculture (Countryside Review Committee, 1977). This decline appears to be losing momentum, but already it is unusual for more than 25 per cent of the workforce to be directly employed on the land even in rural areas.

In visual and land-use terms rural Britain may appear agricultural but its employment structure is now much more diverse. The employment accessibility problem derives in part from the fact that many of the manufacturing, and more especially service, jobs that have taken up the slack are in fact to be found in urban centres, albeit within the broadly defined rural regions. Retailing and to a lesser extent employment are predominantly private sector activities. That is to say they are only weakly susceptible to public planning: the planner can permit such development and can prevent it in places deemed unsuitable, but he cannot direct it to places which are unattractive to the firm in question. In contrast, public sector services are, in principle at least, much more amenable to being steered to locations which are desirable in welfare terms. Below we consider two such services — primary education and medical care.

A basic statistic is that in 1963 34 per cent of British *primary schools* had fewer than 100 pupils, while in 1973 the proportion had fallen to 22 per cent. The small village school is gradually being phased out. In Norfolk, 80 small primary schools closed in the period 1951-71, so that in the early 1970s about 40 per cent of the county's parishes did not have a school (Norfolk County Council 1977). Two main arguments underlie this kind of policy: the economic argument is that average costs — costs per pupil — are higher in smaller schools with labour costs being particularly notable. Work in Scotland by Cumming (1971) confirms this, as does the Norfolk evidence examined in the UEA study. Second, on educational grounds it is argued that children benefit from a diversity of teachers, subjects and equipment which is not easily provided in a small school. The counter-argument that the village school teacher, working alone or with only one colleague, can often achieve great things with a young child whom he or she knows well, may itself be countered with the question — what if that single teacher is a *bad* teacher?

But it is certainly true that the closure of village schools on economic or narrowly defined educational grounds often ignores important social issues. These relate to the role of the school as a focus of community life, to the desirability of educating young children in a familiar environment and to the various social costs imposed upon the family by long-distance travelling to school. For example, there is some evidence (Lee, 1957) that amongst primary school children in rural areas those with long journeys to school have a greater tendency to display signs of personality maladjustment.

Looking ahead, we may briefly cite the long-term education plan approved by the Norfolk County Council in 1975. This plan envisages the closure of about 70 more village schools, mostly with fewer than 50 pupils, by the end of the century. A new pattern of education is slowly being introduced, based on 'middle schools' each with at least 250 8-12 year olds and serving a population catchment of 4000-7000. Popular opposition and the costs of building new schools are tempering this transformation, but again the clear trend of 'bigger, fewer and more widely spaced' is apparent and it is to the access implications of this that we shall later return.

Finally, *medical services*. In primary medical care the tendency for doctors to join together into 'group practices' with at least three members has found expression in the overall reduction in the number of villages having a resident doctor. In 1963 there were 115 doctors' surgeries in rural Norfolk, in 1975 there were 98. Similarly, in 1961 there were 97 village-based child health clinics in the same area; in 1974 there were only 62 (Norfolk County Council, 1977). Further spatial concentration is in train with the establishment of 'health centres' combining surgery facilities for general practice with ancillary medical activities such as the child clinic and dental services. This attempt to draw into a single building the various elements of primary health care is superficially attractive in terms of the advantages of a common administrative staff, the possibility for the patient of making 'multi-purpose medical trips', etc. — but catchment populations of 6000-18,000 are envisaged in Norfolk and this implies quite long journeys for many people.

Concerning hospital services, the trend in the last 10-15 years has been to concentrate most facilities into a small number of 'district general hospitals', each serving around 250,000 people and in rural areas extending their hinterland over a 20-30 mile radius. Again there are clear medical advantages in having the full range of specialist facilities available under one roof: but equally there are parallel problems of access for patients, visitors and staff who do not have ready use of a car. This problem has been noted officially: a DHSS Circular of 1974 stressed the attractions of 'community hospitals' which would serve only 30-100,000 people and hence be at a much more local level (Department of Health and Social Security, 1974). These would be staffed principally by general practitioners, but would also provide facilities for some out-patient work by specialists. In practice many beds would be filled by elderly patients or perhaps by people recovering from an operation at a 'half-way house' between their home and the 'proper' hospital. All-important visiting by friends and relations would be much easier. (Research at the University of East Anglia is actively considering the suitability of a community hospital policy for rural Norfolk — Haynes *et al.* 1978.)

Transport

How has the mobility — actual and potential — of the rural resident changed in recent years? And what does the future hold? The crucial factor, which has of course also substantially affected the location of people and of the facilities to which they require access, has been the rapid rise of the motor car to become the principal mode of transport for most rural households.

The past, present and officially forecast levels of car ownership for Britain as a whole are as follows:

1951	0.05 cars per person
1975	0.25 cars per person
1990	0.38 cars per person
2000	0.44 cars per person

Source: Department of Environment, 1976

The last figure is deemed to be effectively the 'saturation level', dictated by age-structure and other factors. Obviously the forecasts set out above are only informed speculation but they are in line with more recent forecasts produced by the Transport and Road Research Laboratory (Tanner, 1977). The assumptions upon which they were made were the 'pessimistic' ones of an annual growth in GNP of 2½ per cent and a continuing rise of petrol prices in real terms. Less pessimistic assumptions would point to a more substantial rise in car ownership. Real income levels are the prime determinant of the rate of growth of car ownership, although it is interesting that when viewed geographically car ownership is particularly high in many of the poorer counties. To be more precise, car ownership levels tend to correlate positively with a county's average household income and negatively with its population density, with the latter factor being statistically the more significant (Rhys and Buxton, 1974).

Thus even relatively poor, rural counties have high car ownership levels (figure 2.3) — doubtless a response to their basic
accessibility problems, and suggesting a degree of 'reluctant
ownership'.

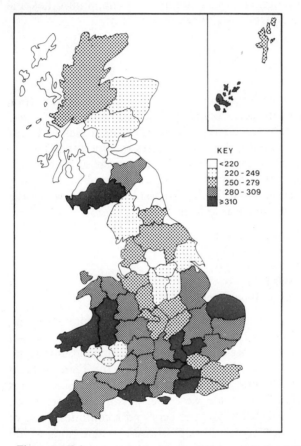

KEY

	<220
	220 - 249
	250 - 279
	280 - 309
	≥310

Figure 2.3 Private cars and vans per 1000 population 1976
Source: 'Transport statistics, Great Britain 1966-76', H.M.S.O. 1978

Expressed in terms of the proportion of households having at
least one car, the national level of car ownership was 56 per cent
in 1976 (Department of Transport, 1978a). But in rural areas the
figure is typically 10-20 percentage points higher (Department of
Environment, 1976). As a corollary, of course, this means that in

rural Britain between one-quarter and one-third of all households lack a car. And while nationally car ownership is likely to continue to rise substantially, in rural areas we may already be quite near an effective ceiling. Not only is the level already high but the household incomes of those without a car is low (the UEA study of rural households in 1975 indicated an average income of £1150 for carless households), and the proportion of elderly residents is high and rising. All this suggests that the car has brought major benefits to the majority of rural households but that there is, and will remain, a substantial number without.

In its comfort, speed, flexibility in routeing and flexibility of timing the car is eminently preferable to the bus in rural areas. And if more than one person travels it is generally more economic to the user. The marginal cost of motoring is still quite low: once a car has been purchased it generally pays to use it rather than any other mode. Indeed, British rural areas are eminently good 'car country', with their dense network of generally well-maintained roads, the lack of problems relating to parking, garaging or congestion, and the generally lower operating costs of rural motoring. No rural transport planner can ignore these advantages: exhortations to motorists to use their rural bus service are doomed to failure because there is really no contest between the two modes, even if both are available.

And, of course, the gap has been widening. As car ownership and car usage have increased in rural areas, so the quality of public transport has declined. The following data on passenger transport in Great Britain as a whole illustrate what has happened nationally:

Mode	1954		1964		1974	
	no.	%	no.	%	no.	%
private road	76	39	213	67	350	79
rail	39	20	37	12	36	8
bus and coach	81	41	65	21	54	12
Total	196	100	315	100	440	100

Data are in '000 million passenger miles.
Source: Department of Environment, 1976

The table shows that movement by whatever mode more than doubled in the 20-year period, while that by car more than quadrupled. Travel by rail remained roughly constant in absolute terms, but that by bus or coach declined substantially. The dramatic way in which the use of public transport has fallen, as car ownership has risen, is shown in figure 2.4.

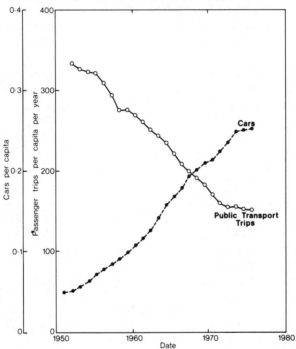

Figure 2.4 Car ownership and public road transport passenger trips in Great Britain
Source: Mitchell (1976), based on National Travel Survey and other evidence

Obviously the factors involved in this are much too complex to be expressed in a couple of paragraphs, but it is undeniable that there is a clear two-way causal link between the rise of car usage and the decline of public transport. A simple model of this cumulative process may be set out in diagrammatic form:

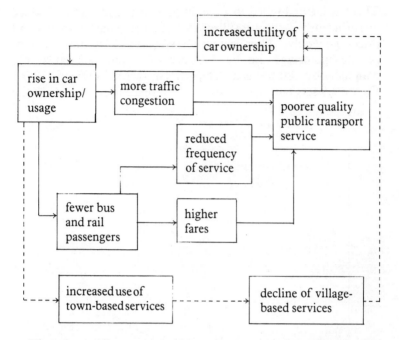

The above diagram is, of course, an over-simplification: in rural areas the 'congestion' link in the system is a weak one, and rising fares can only in part be attributed to declining patronage. But the *cumulative* nature of the problem is the central point, and to this end note the twist to the spiral effected by the decline of village-based services (indicated by broken lines).

Rural bus services have contracted substantially from their heyday in the early 1950s. Typically the vehicle mileage of rural bus operators has declined by about 1 per cent per annum. Thus the decline in Norfolk, between 1954 and 1974, of services run by the main operator was of the order of 25 per cent; that of Western National, between 1960 and 1970, in Devon was about 10 per cent (Department of Environment, 1971a). The private sector has similarly been hit: good data on vehicle mileage are not available, but Clout *et al.* (1972) noted that of the 66 independent bus operators in North Norfolk in 1955 only 46 remained in 1971.

The decline in passenger miles has been greater than that in vehicle miles; in other words the buses have become emptier.

This has inevitably led to a rise in unit costs and, in the absence of sufficiently large subsidies, to fares rising faster than retail prices generally. Thus between 1964 and 1975 the costs of private motoring rose by 140 per cent, but bus fares rose nationally by 180 per cent (Department of Environment, 1976). Figure 2.5 sets out the picture over a rather longer period. In the

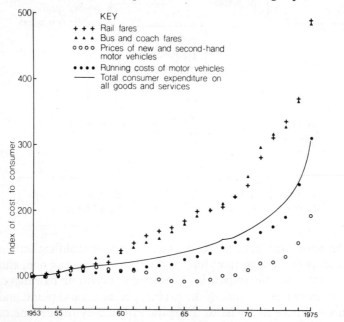

Figure 2.5 Personal transport: indices of costs to the consumer at current prices (1953 = 100)
Source: Owens (1978), after 'Passenger transport in Great Britain', . H.M.S.O. annually

early days operators were able, indeed required by the Traffic Commissioners, to subsidize their loss-making rural services from the proceeds of their profitable urban services, but more recent difficulties with the latter have now virtually removed this possibility. And so, as revenue has fallen, operators have had to respond by raising fares, reducing service quality and, in the 1970s, by seeking subsidies from the county councils. In the future, costs are likely to continue to rise substantially: this is, after all, a labour intensive industry in which wages and salaries account for about three-quarters of all costs. There is only limited scope for cost-cutting: one-man operated services, for example, have already been widely introduced. And because peak-hour services effectively determine the size both of the vehicle fleet and of the labour force, further contraction of off-peak services would bring only modest cost reductions. Similarly the introduction of smaller vehicles — seemingly common sense in a rural context — is generally unattractive given the two points made above: the need for large vehicles anyway for peak-hour services, and the overriding importance of wages in the cost structure. In short, bus operators are and will remain in an invidious position. It *is* still possible, contrary to popular opinion, to raise revenue by raising fares (to use the jargon of the economist, price elasticity is less than unity) and to cut costs by cutting services — but is this downward spiral really in society's best interests?

The decline of the rural rail network has, of course, been even more dramatic. In the 1960s about 5000 miles of passenger-carrying rural railways were lost. Today, outside the Greater London area, nearly all railways have an essentially inter-urban function — the rural branch line is a thing of the past. Taking the 1950s and 1960s together — because the process of decline was certainly in gear well before the descent of the Beeching axe in the early 1960s — Norfolk, for instance, lost 70 per cent of its rail network (figure 2.6). While it is true that the vast majority of rural villages have never had a railway station and that any move to channel resources into reopening closed branch lines would effectively discriminate against their residents, what this decline means is that the inter-small-town rail network has been destroyed. The possibility of building a 'feeder' road transport system on to this basic network no longer exists in most of rural Britain.

Public expenditure

A fourth area of change which affects the accessibility enjoyed by rural residents concerns the ability and willingness of society to purchase solutions to the problems arising from the decline of public transport and the retraction of many rural services. The early 1970s were a period of economic growth, of public

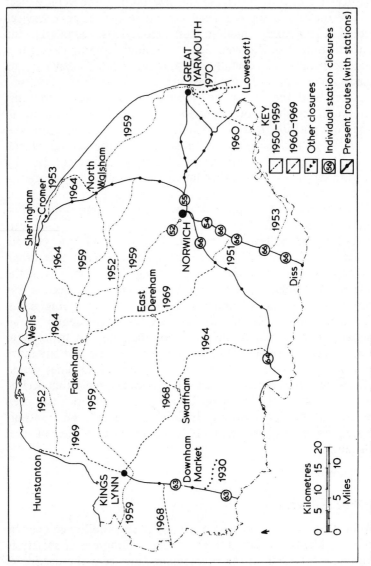

Figure 2.6 Post-war rail closures in Norfolk

expenditure increasing more quickly than GNP and of local authority expenditure rising very substantially. Thus in the five-year period 1970-1 to 1975-6, the gross national product grew by 8 per cent, and total local authority expenditure by 35 per cent. But measures taken by the government in 1975-6, in the wake of the energy crisis of 1974 and in the conviction that investment in manufacturing industry should be given higher priority, sought to contain public sector spending much more effectively. And the Labour government of the mid-1970s has systematically aimed to direct a larger share of public expenditure to the major urban areas where the intensity of many social, economic and environmental problems appears greater. Thus, a much greater proportion of the rate support grant, which amounts to over £6000 million annually and meets well over half of total local authority expenditure, is now directed to London and the other big conurbations at the expense of the non-metropolitan or 'shire' counties which contain virtually all the rural areas — this despite the former's declining population.

Table 2.1 *Shares of the total rate support grant*

Area	1974-5	1978-9
Greater London	16.5%	21.6%
Metropolitan counties and districts	25.3%	26.5%
Shire counties and districts	58.2%	51.9%
	100.0%	100.0%

Source: Jackman, 1978

The 'Inner Cities' white paper (Department of Environment, 1977) foreshadows further shifts of resources in favour of the big cities, not only in the rate support grant allocation but in other areas of government expenditure which will be given 'an inner urban dimension and priority'. It may well be that the conurbations' problems are more severe than those of the rural areas — to assess their relative severity is beyond the scope of this book —

but the accessibility problems of the latter are real enough and the adverse trends in public expenditure provide another element of the context within which their resolution has to be sought. One further point must be made about public expenditure as it affects rural areas. Consequent upon the radical re-examination of spending priorities which occurred in the mid-1970s, and more specifically upon the review of transport policy which occurred at the same time, an increasing proportion of transport-related public expenditure now goes towards the support of public transport rather than the building and maintenance of roads (table 2.2).

Table 2.2 *Inland surface transport public expenditure** (£m at 1976 prices)

Some major heads	1971-2	1973-4	1976-7	End of decade (proposed in White Paper)
Motorways and trunk roads				
(i) construction	485	495	460	380
(ii) maintenance	65	100	80	80
Local transport				
(i) roads and car parks capital expenditure	525	565	370	260
(ii) roads maintenance	480	485	440	400
Central govt support of British rail passenger services	135	250	325	295
Local govt current subsidies to buses, rail etc.	10	40	210	185
Other	340	425	735	600
Total	2,040	2,360	2,620	2,200

*Excluding investment by nationalized surface transport industries
Source: Transport 'White Paper' (Department of Transport, 1977)

And the government has expressed its intention to give some priority to rural areas in the allocation of money intended for bus revenue support (Department of Transport, 1978b). But the latest public expenditure pronouncement (H.M. Treasury, 1978) indicates that the total resources available for public transport must remain roughly constant into the early 1980s.

In other words, in so far as there is a government policy for expenditure in the rural areas (and it is never articulated in these terms) there is a tendency towards increased support for rural public transport, but this is more than offset by an overall government shift of resources to the major urban areas. One final point: central government holds only part, albeit a large part, of the purse strings. What local authorities decide is also important and the general tendency is for rural (or 'shire') county and district councils to hold down expenditure as far as they are able. Thus in 1976-7 while the London councils spent on average £268 per head of population on all their services and the metropolitan councils £223, the shire counties spent only £192 (CIPFA Return of Rates, 1976-7). This can only partly be explained by central government's reluctance to advance them grants or loans. It derives also from a general reluctance of predominantly conservative controlled councils to spend their residents' money on public services. Whether this is a 'good' or 'bad' thing is obviously a matter of opinion: the point is simply that in considering how rural areas will develop, the financial/political dimension is an important one.

3
Mobility deprivation

The rural accessibility system, then, is in a state of flux. The rural population is changing in numbers and in composition; the car has increased the mobility of some while declining public transport has worsened that of others; the goals of transport — the shops, schools and workplaces to which trips are made — are becoming fewer in number and more widely spaced. This chapter examines some of the inequities which result from these changes. In particular, who enjoys the mobility that higher levels of car ownership imply? And who suffers most from the deterioration of public transport? If mobility is 'the capacity that a person has for getting around' (Hillman *et al.*, 1973), then who is deprived of this capacity? First, however, we consider the withdrawal of public transport (and of fixed-location services such as shops) as a 'force for change' and ask whether it is possible to establish the ripples of further change that such forces bring about in rural areas.

Response to change

What happens when a bus service is withdrawn or a village shop closed? How do people manage? How do they change their lives? What happens to their village? A similar set of questions needs to be asked about hypothetical *possible* changes: if this or that bus service were to be withdrawn, or if this or that shop or school were closed what would be the effect upon people's well-being and upon community life?

Unfortunately it is not easy to answer such questions with any precision. Two extreme positions are tenable. First, one can assume that everyone quickly and adequately adapts to changing circumstances. A study by the Department of Environment (1971a) of the situation in parts of rural Devon concluded that 'clearly people have adapted to the absence of a bus; those who could not presumably left some time ago. Those who have moved in, including retired people, have cars.' Alternatively all of the various problems of rural areas can be, and sometimes have been, laid at the door of the disappearing public transport system. Thus the exodus of young people and the ageing of the community, the decline in the number of jobs and the difficulty of their replacement, high unemployment and low female activity rates, boredom and disaffection amongst youth and loneliness amongst the elderly, the transformation of 'viable' communities into havens for the urban middle classes — all have at some time been attributed to the demise of the rural bus! The analytical problem is first of all to discover just what change has been occurring and then to establish how the various elements of change are linked by causal connections.

Consider, for example, the depopulation which has been a feature of many of the remoter rural areas. Does it *cause* a decline in public transport by reducing the latter's market, or is it *caused* by transport decline as people move out to escape their problems of immobility? Almost certainly the answer to both questions is 'yes to some extent'. But to what extent? And maybe there are 'third forces' involved which contribute *both* to depopulation *and* to worsening transport — for example a general decline in job opportunities in rural areas.

With reference to the diagram below, a number of questions might be asked.

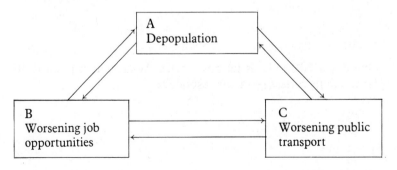

(i) Should there in fact be *six* arrows included? Which ones might be excluded as being relatively unimportant?

(ii) What is the *relative* strength of the arrow which links worsening public transport to depopulation? Is it really important?

(iii) In a more sophisticated model of the causes of depopulation, or of the consequences of worsening public transport, what *other* factors should be incorporated?

It must be stressed that the simple 'system' outlined above is introduced only by way of illustration — to demonstrate the dangers of jumping to conclusions of cause and effect. The basic point is that 'everything affects everything else' and that the analyst must try to establish the nature and the relative strength of those effects. In fact he should ideally build some sort of model which encapsulates them. Unfortunately we are a long way from having such a model of rural change, though there are partial elements which will be introduced at appropriate points in this book. Suffice it to say here that policy decisions presuppose a prior knowledge of the intricacies of the rural accessibility system: by taking a decision, say, to re-route a bus service, or to replace a fixed library by a mobile library, or to grant permissions for residential development in only a few chosen centres, the policy maker is hypothesizing that people's behaviour will be modified in ways that, in aggregate, are beneficial. This hypothesis may often be largely a matter of informed judgement and faith.

Perhaps, however, this is too gloomy a view of our knowledge of the processes of rural change. Let us try, in fact, to establish what sort of reactions are most likely given one particularly relevant impulse for change — the loss of a bus service serving a particular village. How will people probably react? First we shall outline their options and then we shall review the empirical evidence provided by a number of recent studies.

1 THE OPTIONS

One day a village loses its bus service. What will happen to it? How will its carless residents respond?

(i) *Migrate*

The most drastic possibility is for people without the use of a car to leave the village and move to some other place which retains its bus service or where its absence is less keenly felt. If the whole household moves rather than just one affected member, then this involves the vacation of a house and its eventual reoccupation by a new household (perhaps on a 'second home' basis) which is likely to have the means of overcoming the immobility brought about by the bus service withdrawal, or else to attach less importance to such immobility.

(ii) *Make alternative transport arrangements*

An alternative is for carless residents to remain in the village but to travel by a different means of transport. The purchase of a motorcar, motorcycle or cycle becomes more likely, or the use of some alternative transport service. Arrangements might be made with a neighbour to get a life occasionally, or the need might be accepted to walk some distance to get a bus from another village. If alternative transport arrangements are made the pattern of trip-making might itself change: the purchase of a car might lead, for example, to once-fortnightly shopping in a major centre rather than twice weekly trips to the market town. Further effects might ensue from this (see diagram p.21).

(iii) *Increase village-based activities*

The third option is to accept the enforced immobility and to reduce the amount of trip-making. Greater use could be made of the village shop, if there is one. Mail-order shopping could replace longer distance shopping trips. The use of television and perhaps the telephone could increase to offset the inability to make social and recreational trips.

These three options subsume most of the possibilities, but in addition there is what might be termed the response of the *village 'community'* as a whole. The residents could react collectively by pressing the authorities to restore the service or to provide some compensatory facility. And the nature of the community could itself change as a consequence of the various individual decisions set out above under (i), (ii) and (iii). The village could become more car-dominated, either through the residents buying their own or through car-owning people moving in. It could decline in population as disaffected people leave and are not replaced. It could become a second-home or retirement community for the urban middle-classes.

Parallel to these hypothesized reactions by the residents and by the village commmunity, are possible responses by the *providers of services*, whether in the public or private sector. The village shopkeeper might enjoy an increase in .business from his now captive clientele (or a decline in business if the now severed bus service once brought him customers from afar). Traders elsewhere might choose to run a mobile or delivery service into the village or even (as in the case of Cromer shopkeepers seeking the business of certain villagers in north Norfolk) provide transport to draw in their customers from the vicinity. Decisions by employers to lay on a 'work's bus', by the local authority to provide a school bus and a mobile library, or by the local medical practice to open a 'branch surgery' in the village may all be seen as outside responses to the loss of the village's bus service.

Similar categories of response could be set out for possible responses to the loss not of a bus service but of a village shop, school, pub or post office. Any such impulse for change is likely to generate changes in the behaviour of a wide range of people. The difficulty is to know what sort of change is most likely, what 'second-round' effects will ensue thereafter — most important from a planning viewpoint — how much of this change may reasonably be considered to be unacceptable to society. When does a 'behavioural adaptation constitute a mile and passing inconvenience and when a genuine source of hardship?

2 THE EVIDENCE

The view that the loss of rural public transport services is a major factor in stimulating depopulation is not supported by the available evidence. Studies in Britain and Ireland (e.g., Jansen, 1968; 1969; Hannan, 1969) indicate that a resident's propensity to leave a rural location is related chiefly to demographic factors (notably his or her age, sex, marital status and size of family) and to the gap between the person's aspirations and the local opportunities available to attain those aspirations. Rural out-migration is a response chiefly to a feeling of 'dislocation from the local community and the strength of social and economic aspirations' (Hannan, 1969).

A number of attempts have in fact been made to establish a correlation between poor service provision in a village (whether fixed-location services or transport services) and levels of out-migration from the village — but generally without success. For example Clout *et al.* (1973) examined 100 parishes in north Norfolk to see whether their increase or decrease in population in the 1950s and 1960s was in any way related to changes they experienced in the quality of their bus services: no correlation was found. Similarly in the UEA study the fortunes in the 1960s of 25 mid-Norfolk parishes which had lost their rail services in 1959 were examined. The subsequent changes observed in their total population, type of population and level of car ownership did not differ significantly from those observed in a similar set of parishes which had not suffered a sudden decline in public transport provision.

All this suggests that a decline in the quality and availability of public transport is at most a weak force in the demographic changes affecting rural areas: it does not set in motion significant migratory movements. But perhaps this should itself be a cause for concern: any hardship brought about appears to find expression in other ways with the disadvantaged people remaining in the rural areas and 'coping' in some way.

The Department of Environment studies (1971a and b) of parts of Devon and west Suffolk each tried to establish how people managed their lives in busless villages. The Devon village of Spreyton had lost the last vestige of its bus service five years previously. The researchers found that 90 per cent of households had a car and that there was a good deal of informal lift-giving in operation. The main effect had apparently been to reduce the ability of many Spreyton residents to make shopping or social trips out of the village. The west Suffolk hamlet of Somerton, which had lost its bus service eight years before the study and was two miles from the nearest bus route, showed a variety of features which were attributed to its inaccessibility — a high proportion of second homes, pensioners being allowed to travel on the school bus, considerable use of bicycles by pensioners and an informal system of lift-giving. In both Devon and Suffolk studies the authors concluded that very few potential trips were apparently frustrated through lack of transport.

A more recent study by Helling (1976) reached less sanguine conclusions. He studied three hamlets in Hertfordshire, Buckinghamshire and Tayside which had lost their bus services a year or so before. He found *some* evidence of migration to better served places and of households reluctantly buying a car. More significant was a reduction in the number of visitors coming to call on their friends, and in the frequency and convenience of trips to town. Some respondents recounted that they had to spend long hours away from home waiting for alternative transport to bring them home. Others said that they had increased their use of taxis, mobile services and lifts in other people's cars — usually those of relatives rather than friends. Helling concluded that

> overall, the general picture is of a relatively small but significant number of people being forced to suffer increased inconvenience and difficulty in their lives, and, for some, a reduction in their social lives and increased isolation from friends and relatives. Very few people had been able to arrange much in the way of adequate alternatives to the buses. On this showing, bus service cuts will have little effect on the volume of cars on the roads, but can cause a significant deterioration in the quality of life for former users, especially the elderly and those in areas remote from other public transport.

The UEA study tried in two ways to establish how Norfolk people have reacted to the decline in public transport in their area. Over 600 households were asked directly about how the cuts had affected them and, in a second study, a member of the research team lived for a fortnight in two small villages, asking long-established residents about a variety of changes occurring in the previous 20 years.

The household surveys were carried out in areas where, in general terms, the deterioration in public transport services had been modest but prolonged. About one-third of the respondents perceived that 'public transport in this part of Norfolk is not as good as it was about five years ago'. Of all the respondents about 17 per cent perceived some effect of these changes upon their household, and 7-8 per cent said that the effects amounted to 'quite severe inconvenience or hardship'. About 16 per cent of the respondents reported some behavioural change arising from the decline in the bus services — about 23 per cent of carless households. The most frequently reported change was 'go out less/reduced freedom of movement', but a few respondents referred to a 'modal change' — they walked or cycled more or had bought a car. Others referred to the difficulties of reaching specific services — shops, hairdressers, doctors, surgeries and children's activities.

Rather fewer respondents (20-5 per cent) perceived a decline in 'fixed-location services' in their area — defined as 'shops, schools, pubs, post offices, etc.' Only 10 per cent perceived some effect upon the household, and this amounted to 'quite severe inconvenience or hardship' for only 2-3 per cent of respondents. In most cases it was the greater difficulty, expense and distance of shopping trips that was the source of concern.

Respondents were also asked in what ways, if any, the general decline in public transport and service provision was affecting their village as a whole. About 60 per cent claimed to perceive effects upon their village. Curiously, roughly equal numbers felt that general levels of access had increased or had decreased, depending on the view held about the consequence of higher levels of car ownership. But many did observe greater hardship for the elderly, more communal help, for example lift-giving, than hitherto and much greater reliance on the private car. Two other effects were frequently perceived, which might in fact be only very partially the responsibility of worsening public transport, namely the breakdown of the village as a social unit and a rapid influx of newcomers into the village.

The second study involved a researcher living temporarily in Trunch and Southrepps, two small villages about five miles from the north Norfolk coast. A careful analysis of bus timetables for 1956, 1965 and 1975 had revealed modest deterioration of public transport in Trunch and substantial deterioration in Southrepps, especially in the frequency of services to the small towns of Cromer and North Walsham and to Norwich, but what transport-related behavioural changes occurred in the twenty-year period?

Regarding *employment*, the major change in these two villages had been a shift from local farmwork reached on foot or by bicycle, to more distant factory and office employment reached by car: public transport had never been particularly important for the work trip. The greater difficulty of making shopping trips by bus had been largely offset by the retention in each village of at least one general store, by the high level of car ownership, and by an attractive innovatory free bus service into the villages provided once weekly by Cromer traders. The inability to make *social or recreation* trips by bus, for example to the cinema, appeared of little concern to most people with a car and television. But teenagers seemed to suffer, and here rising expectations were clearly important: twenty years ago a 17-year old would have happily cycled four miles to a dance in North Walsham, but by 1975 this was apparently socially unacceptable. It was access to *medical facilities* that was the greatest cause for concern. Doctors were apparently ready to visit patients if access problems were particularly severe and one practice held a once-weekly branch surgery in Southrepps. Lifts were readily offered and accepted if someone was ill, but routine trips to the doctor or chemist or to visit a friend in hospital posed problems.

In conclusion, the decline of public transport and of service provision has been only one force, a relatively weak force, in bringing about the far-reaching social and economic transformation of post-war rural Britain. Typically, rural residents have reacted to change by means of a variety of *ad hoc* low key responses. Cars have become more plentiful and more frequently used by their owners and, often, for the benefit of others. Many doctors, retailers, local authorities and others responsible for the provision of services have attempted to make some adjustment in their affairs to accommodate the carless. But it is undeniable that a minority of households has been affected in a manner which amounts to hardship. Increased inconvenience and isolation have resulted for many people, and to a degree that public agencies have as yet been unable or unwilling to alleviate.

Mobility today: the motor car and its substitutes

So far we have considered the development of the rural accessibility problem, and of popular responses to it. It is useful to know how circumstances have changed through time, but ultimately the measure of the problem must be not how people fare in relation to some historical yardstick but how their circumstances compare with some presently acceptable standard. What are the disparities *today* between the haves and have-nots of rural mobility? It is with this question that the remainder of the chapter is concerned. First we examine the availability of the motor car, the bus and the telephone. Then, in the final section, the circumstances of specific disadvantaged social groups are described.

1 CAR AVAILABILITY

The lack of a car is probably the biggest single factor in any identification of those rural people who are disadvantaged in access terms. Who are they? Why do they lack a car? And how is their behaviour affected?

We have already noted that car ownership levels are typically high in rural Britain — the proportion varies from place to place, but around 70 per cent of rural households have at least one car. Those households with two or more amount to 15-20 per cent of the total. Household income is the prime determinant of car ownership. In the UEA survey of 634 rural households only 8 per cent of those households with an income of more than £2000 per annum in 1975 had no car. (The national average household income in 1975 was over £3000 — *Social Trends*, 1976.) Car ownership levels were high amongst quite low-income households, and the reported average income of carless households was only £1150. Figure 3.1 indicates the number of households with zero, one or two-plus cars, by income bracket. (The sample size was small and so undue reliance should not be placed on individual points on the curves but the overall pattern is likely to be valid.)

It is clear that many of the poorer households must make considerable sacrifices in other areas to be able to buy and run a car. A A study of *Low pay on the farm* by Brown and Winyard (1975) revealed that some rural families go without breakfast and buy their clothes in jumble sales in order to run a car. Clearly car ownership has become a painful necessity. One respondent remarked 'What man in his right mind would try to run a car on

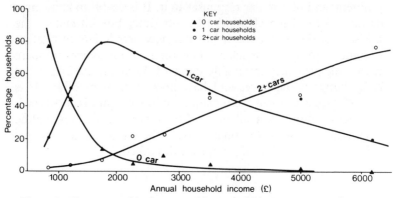

Figure 3.1 Car ownership by annual household income: parts of rural Norfolk 1975
Source: survey evidence reported in Moseley *et al.* (1977)

my wage (£29.50 gross in 1974)? But living here, ten miles from the nearest town, I have no choice.' Another man, whose wife was a diabetic in need of frequent medical treatment, explained: 'I have to keep a gallon of petrol in the car for emergencies. We never use the car for pleasure, just for essential shopping trips or trips to the doctor. If we forget anything its just too bad. We can't afford another journey.'

Even so, all the evidence points to the liberating effect of car availability. And it must be stressed that it is car availability, not car ownership that is crucial. Within car-owning households there are usually people who are effectively denied use of the car for much of the time. Part of the problem is licence holding. Data from the 1972-3 National Travel Survey indicate that at that time 26 per cent of the population was too young to hold a driving licence, and of those aged over 17 years, only 64 per cent of men and 21 per cent of women had a licence. Age and social class — as well as sex — are key factors. Amongst women only 4 per cent of those over 65 years held a licence, and only 7 per cent of those in unskilled and skilled manual occupations.

In the UEA study, all adult household members were placed into one of four mobility groups:

No driving licence:	41% of all adults
Driving licence, but never has a car to drive:	5% of all adults
Driving licence, but rarely has a car to drive:	6% of all adults
Driving licence and nearly always has a car to drive:	48% of all adults

Considering in more detail membership of the fourth, most mobile, category it should be stated that it includes:

> 0% of all children (under 17 years)
> only 25% of all elderly people (over 65 years)
> only 30% of all women
> but 73% of all married men

Hillman's study (1973) of a rural parish in Oxfordshire gave very similar results. Categorizing the various adult members of the two hundred households surveyed, according to whether they had a driving licence and whether their household had a car, he arrived at the following results:

	All adults	All men	All women	All pensioners
Car-owning households				
(i) licence-holders	48%	67%	33%	24%
(ii) non-licence-holders	20%	6%	31%	18%
Non-car-owning households				
(iii) licence-holders	5%	8%	2%	0%
(iv) non-licence-holders	28%	20%	34%	58%
	100%	100%	100%	100%

Individual cells in the above table are based on small absolute figures, but a marked contrast in car availability by sex and age comes out clearly.

What is more the inequalities apparent in studies of licence-holding are compounded by the frequent pre-emption of the household car by an individual household member. Typically this happens when the husband chooses or has to use the car for the journey to work, leaving his wife and family without the vehicle for much of the day.

In short there are really three categories of rural people in terms of their basic mobility endowment:

(i)   those with a car generally available for their use;
(ii) those in car-owning households but not in category (i);
(iii) those not in car-owning households.

Rural accessibility planning should properly be directed at alleviating the problems of categories (ii) and (iii). Three particular groups of people fall into these categories: first, the elderly; second, children and teenagers; third, economically inactive married women (or 'housewives') not in two-car households. In addition, and overlapping, are the poor, whether male or female, and the disabled. Collectively these people comprise the *majority* of the rural population. The view that the rural accessibility problem affects only a 'residual minority' is a myth.

2 BUS AVAILABILITY, QUALITY AND USE

In the absence of private transport, how far does public transport fill the gap? Inevitably its quality varies considerably both between counties and, more significantly, within counties. A survey of nine counties in southern England, undertaken by the Association of Transport Coordinating Officers in 1976, yielded the following ranking according to the proportions of each county's parishes having over 100 buses per week. (The proportion of parishes having fewer than 6 buses per week is also shown.)

Area	Parishes with over 100 buses	Parishes with fewer than 6 buses
West Sussex	36.2%	13.0%
Wiltshire	32.5%	17.3%
Warwickshire	29.9%	30.8%
Hampshire	25.6%	15.9%
Oxfordshire	24.6%	21.4%
Leicestershire	24.6%	23.6%
Cambridgeshire	20.3%	16.7%
Northants	17.7%	21.2%
Norfolk	7.5%	35.7%

Care should be taken not to read too much into these figures — the geographical extent of individual parishes will obviously affect the result. But clearly counties such as West Sussex tend to enjoy a much higher general level of service than does Norfolk, for example.

Within counties, disparities are much more marked. A major factor is settlement size: predictably, large villages tend to enjoy better bus services. This emerges clearly in table 3.1 which sets out raw data from which the above county summaries were derived. There are nine matrices in table 3.1, one for each county, and each shows bus frequency (vertical axis) by parish size (horizontal axis), the latter being measured not by means of a crude count of inhabitants, but by the more useful number of carless households. Thus, for example, in Oxfordshire 16 of the smallest parishes (top left cell in the matrix) enjoyed over 100 buses weekly, but 31 of these smallest parishes (bottom left cell) had no bus service at all. Data of this sort provide a basis for inter- and intra-county analyses of service quality. Clearly much of rural Britain has a nonexistent or very rudimentary bus service: on this evidence about one-quarter of all the rural parishes of lowland England have fewer than one bus daily.

But frequency is only one attribute of service quality. Others are fare levels, comfort, reliability and the convenience of timings and of destinations. The evidence is somewhat equivocal on the relative importance of these factors to users. Respondents in the Department of Environment's Devon and west Suffolk surveys (1971a and b) were asked to choose the kind of improvement they would prefer for their local bus service:

44% said greater frequency
21% said lower fares
16% said more convenient routes
 7% said greater reliability

But in the UEA Survey 'reliability', 'frequency' and 'places served' were the greatest causes for complaint about rural bus services. 'Fares' and 'timings' were much less important. (It is interesting that on all five attributes, members of two-car households held a more favourable opinion of the services than did members of one-car households who in turn held a more favourable opinion than did those in no-car households. It seems

Table 3.1 *Bus service frequencies by parish size: an analysis of nine English counties* *

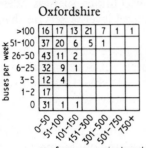

Oxfordshire

buses per week	0-50	51-100	101-150	151-300	301-500	501-750	750+
>100	16	17	13	21	7	1	1
51-100	37	20	6	5	1		
26-50	43	11	2				
6-25	32	9	1				
3-5	12	4					
1-2	17						
0	31	1	1				

no. of non-car-owning households

Norfolk

>100	7	7	4	13	4	1
51-100	49	29	13	8	2	3
26-50	53	38	16	7	1	
6-25	44	9	1	1		
3-5	23	10	2			
1-2	79	13	1			
0	41	2				

Northamptonshire

>100	14	11	5	8	5	3
51-100	20	13	1	4	3	
26-50	49	5	1	2		
6-25	51	7	2	1		
3-5	22					
1-2	11					
0	22					

Warwickshire

28	7	6	9	8	7	1
10	1	9	5			
20	6	1	1			
29	3	1	1			
6	1					
6	1					
51	1	1		*1*		

Leicestershire

10	9	7	13	9	12	8
15	8	3	5	2	1	
26	14	1	2			
57	9					
14	2					
8						
41						

Wiltshire

22	20	9	14	10	5	1
23	8	4	4	1		
32	12		4			
26	10					
17	4					
9	1		1			
12						

Cambridgeshire

12	11	9	8	8	2	1
22	15	9	12	2	1	
16	17	5	5		1	
40	11	3	1			
7	1					
16						
18						

Hampshire

15	9	6	16	7	2	3
16	19	7	6	5	1	1
17	8	6	4			
31	4	1	2			
3		1				
6		1				
22	3					

West Sussex

7	8	9	9	8	5	4
5	6	4	6	3	2	
7	5	4	6			
14	7	1				
7	1					
3	1					
5	1					

*Each cell total indicates a number of parishes.

Source: ATCO (1976); by permission of the Association of Transport Coordinating Officers.

that those who use or most need to use public transport are most critical of its qualities.) But whichever particular factors are most critical, it would seem that the absence and infrequency of bus services *today*, is a factor more relevant to questions of policy than their quality compared with that of some previous heyday.

How much use is actually made of public transport in rural Britain? In the UEA survey only 33% of all respondents had used a bus or train in the preceding month. Both the Devon and West Suffolk studies indicated that only about 6 per cent of rural

Table 3.2 Mode of travel by trip purpose, in rural *West Suffolk and Devon, 1971*

Mode	Work		School		Shopping		Leisure		All trips	
	West Suffolk	Devon	West Suffolk	Devon	West Suffolk	Devon	West Suffolk	Devon	West Suffolk	Devon
Stage bus	6	7	3	8	19	13	3	5	6	6
Works' bus	3	6	-	-	-	-	-	-	1	2
School bus	-	-	61	67	-	-	-	-	8	13
Car or van, (household's or firm's)	66	67	19	16	68	76	75	76	66	66
Borrowed car/ arranged lift	7	10	5	4	6	5	12	11	7	8
Motor cycle or cycle	15	8	5	1	3	1	5	1	8	2
Other (esp. walk, taxi, train)	3	2	7	4	4	6	5	8	4	3
Total	100%	100%	100%	100%	100%	100%	100%	100%	100%	100%

Source: DoE, 1971a and 1971b

residents used public transport on most days of the week. These latter two studies, drawing upon evidence provided by several thousand respondents in 1971, provide the best indication of mode of transport by trip purpose in rural Britain (table 3.2). (The table has been simplified from those in the original reports and it should be explained that work, school, shopping and leisure trips formed about 80 per cent of all trips recorded. Also, the very low incidence of walked trips probably reflects some degree of bias against very local, frequent trips in the question format.) Examining table 3.2, two things stand out: first, the supreme importance of the motorcar as a means of travel; second, the importance of the school bus and of car-sharing, each of which accounts for more trips than do conventional stage-carriage bus services. Further, modal split differs quite considerably between the various trip purposes.

3 TELEPHONE OWNERSHIP, AVAILABILITY AND USE

Perhaps the absence of a motorcar and the imperfection of the bus service can be offset to some extent by the use of the telephone. Trips solely for information or for social contact could be avoided and agencies could be contacted, for example retailers and doctors, with a view to their delivering their service to the house.

In fact only about half of Norfolk's rural households have a telephone, and the figure is rather lower for the more inaccessible parishes outside Norwich's commuter hinterland. There is also, of course, a correlation between income levels and telephone 'ownership'. In the UEA survey only a third of households with an income of less than £2000 p.a. had a phone, compared with over 80 per cent of those earning more than £2000. Not surprisingly, households without a car also tend to lack a phone:

	0 car households	1 car households	2 + cars households	All households
With a phone	22%	55%	81%	52%
Without a phone	78%	45%	19%	48%
Total	100%	100%	100%	100%

Thus, from the above survey, it emerged that four out of five 'two-car' households also have a phone, while a similar proportion of 'no-car' households do not have a phone. At present, then, telephone 'ownership' is a poor substitute for the lack of a car in rural areas.

However, there is evidence that easy access to a neighbour's or to a public telephone can compensate partially for this. Respondents in the UEA study *not* having a telephone were asked whether, *within five minute's walk*, there was a public call box or a friend's or neighbour's telephone that they could use *regularly* (percentages add to over 100 per cent because rows 2 and 3 are not mutually exclusive):

Have telephone in the home	52	per cent of all households
No telephone in home but public telephone available	27	,,
No telephone in home but neighbour's telephone available	22	,,
No telephone access at all	11	,,

Thus, it appears that about 90 per cent of all households have access to a telephone on a regular basis within five minutes' walk of their home. But for many people, of course, this would be for outgoing calls only.

Who suffers mobility deprivation?

1 THE ELDERLY

There are 9.4 million people of pensionable age in Great Britain and this number will show a modest increase at least until the mid-1980s (OPCS 1977). The rural areas are, for reasons discussed in chapter 2, increasingly important as homes for the elderly, and yet in many ways the elderly are poorly adapted to the accessibility problems which such areas present. First, their physical characteristics: nationally, about one-third of those over retirement age have difficulty in seeing and a similar proportion have hearing complaints. A quarter have arthritic complaints, and from the UEA survey, it emerged that about 25 per cent of the elderly had 'serious difficulty in physically moving'. Second, their social characteristics: one-fifth of all elderly people in Britain live alone and even elderly couples can be isolated from their friends and family. Third, income: elderly people tend to be amongst the poorest sections of society. In the UEA study, 55 per cent of households containing exclusively elderly people had an annual income of less than £1000 in 1975.

All this, and deep-seated cultural factors relating to the attitudes and history of the elderly, finds expression in real mobility deprivation. In the UEA study, only about 35 per cent of the rural households composed exclusively of elderly people had a car, and we have already seen that only one-quarter of individual elderly people normally had a car at their disposal. Elderly women are particularly disadvantaged. What frequently happens is that an elderly couple in their sixties retire to a rural area with a car and the money to run it. Then inflation or the physical disability or death of the driver robs the couple, or the surviving member, of the use of the car. Quite quickly what was an attractive rural environment becomes a liability and the house-price gradient which originally attracted the couple from their high-value urban or suburban home, now inhibits their return or the return of the surviving member . A social problem ensues.

So as to help alleviate the mobility problems of the elderly, local authorities are empowered to operate concessionary travel schemes in which bus operators are recompensed for offering fare reductions to this group. A 1976 survey (McTavish, 1978) revealed that 85 per cent of British people over retirement age are eligible for some sort of bus fare concession (there is a wide variety of schemes) but that the vast majority of these live in the major urban areas. Thus 56 per cent of the south west's pensioners and 21 per cent of those living in East Anglia are ineligible. Clearly many rural local authorities place priority upon channelling any expenditure towards maintaining a basic service network, and equally clearly rural concessionary fare schemes do imply a degree of discrimination in favour of those elderly residents who live near good bus routes, but the patchwork pattern of schemes seems to bear no relationship to need and is often a source of resentment amongst those who live on the 'wrong' side of a district council boundary.

Even if a bus service runs quite near to an elderly person's home (and Hillman *et al.* (1976) found that amongst those living in villages in the Outer Metropolitan Area, 26 per cent were more than ten minutes walk from a bus stop) this does not mean that all is well. A five minute walk can be exhausting and elderly people have even greater difficulty returning from the bus stop after a tiring journey and with heavy shopping bags. Often they must wait long periods for a bus without shelter or seating. Boarding and alighting can also pose real problems, especially if the step is high and if the bus is one-man operated. In many ways these are little things, not the stuff of strategic accessibility planning, but they are of very great concern to the people who suffer them. (Garden (1978) provides a recent review of the particular transport problems of the elderly.)

The lack of a car and of a good bus service is often compounded by complementary deficiencies: there is in fact a high degree of 'multiple mobility deprivation' amongst the rural elderly. The UEA study looked at the incidence amongst elderly households of nine factors: no car, no bus in the parish, no shop, someone in the household physically handicapped, income below £1000 p.a., no telephone, no available public or private telephone within five minutes walk, no bicycle, no fridge. Of the carless elderly households, 67 per cent suffered at least three more factors from this list, and 22 per cent suffered at least five more.

And yet elderly people do need to travel. Shops are needed frequently, particularly if the person has no fridge and insufficient money to buy in bulk. The onset of old age means that medical facilities are needed disproportionately often by this group: in the UEA study, one-third of all elderly respondents had had medical treatment in the previous month and many referred to their medical trips as 'fairly or very inconvenient'. The capacity to make social or leisure trips is important and yet in practice car-owning, elderly households make many more such trips. The same study established the proportion of elderly households containing someone who had made certain social trips in the previous month. The results were: to a library, 41 per cent of car-owning households, 19 per cent of non-car-owning households; to a pub, 40 per cent and 22 per cent; to a cinema or theatre 9 per cent and 2 per cent; to visit a friend in hospital 17 per cent and 11 per cent; to visit a friend living outside the village 52 per cent and 27 per cent. Hillman's study of the rural elderly in the Outer Metropolitan Area (Hillman, 1976) confirms the isolation that this implies. Over half of his 'village pensioners' made no social trips and one-quarter received no social visits in an average week — proportions which were significantly higher than those of their urban counterparts.

Some of the human implications of the immobility of the rural elderly were brought out in a survey carried out, in 1971 by Age Concern, of 117 old people's clubs in rural Britain (Age Concern, 1973). The chief sources of complaint about the transport services were first, the withdrawal or non-existence of services; second the high fares; and third the design of the vehicles, with the step height and location of seats being particularly mentioned. Since 1971 the first two of these characteristics has deteriorated further in many areas, but it is salutary to consider the comment of one respondent from Staffordshire: 'To visit our old members in hospital costs 70 pence [in 1971]. This means that their old friends cannot afford to visit them. This is a tragedy: I feel the clasp of a hand means so much more than a letter probably written and read secondhand.' Another respondent, this time from Berkshire, drew attention to the inconvenience and expense of trips to town:

> This is a hamlet where there is now no post office or shop of any kind. The only bus service is to a large town eight miles away — 8 a.m. there and return at 5.40 p.m. except on Thursdays when a bus returns at approximately 10 a.m. This is used by pensioners but costs them 30 pence return [in 1971]. Only those who are compelled to go use this service, because it is too expensive apart from being inconvenient. A day in town is too long for them, as to spend time in a town costs money.

All surveys of the mobility and accessibility problems of people living in rural areas point to the elderly being the single most important disadvantaged group. Studies both of how they actually behave and of the opportunities afforded to them by their 'environment' of cars, buses and other services point to the severity of their disadvantage. And yet how many rural plans — whether physical, transport or social plans — explicitly include the welfare of the elderly as an objective whose degree of attainment is to be carefully sought and then monitored? In the Age Concern survey, referred to above, one respondent shrewdly observed that 'old people now bear the burden of the changes of travel fashions made possible by a prosperity for which they laid the foundations' — yet rural planners are far from clear about how this injustice should be corrected.

2 CHILDREN AND TEENAGERS

Another group which is disadvantaged in mobility terms in rural areas are young people. Admittedly the journey to school is not normally a serious problem for them. The 1944 Education Act imposed upon local education authorities the duty of ensuring the provision of, and of paying for, adequate transport to school for all children living over three miles from their school (two miles in the case of children under eight years). But this is not to say that many shorter school trips do not cause anxiety and inconvenience to parents: the UEA survey revealed great concern at the dangers of young children walking along narrow, unlit rural roads, as well as the inconvenience experienced by adults in accompanying children to and from school, whether on foot or by car.

Hillman *et al.* (1973; 1976) has stressed young people's increasing need for independence of movement as they grow older: they need to be able to travel so as to explore their external environment and to assert their identity outside the family. Particularly relevant constraints which impede their mobility in rural areas include parental reluctance to provide a chauffeur service, the paucity of public transport in the evenings, and peer group pressure which makes teenagers feel that they have 'grown out of riding a bike'.

Both Hillman's work and the UEA study point to the particular difficulties inhibiting participation in evening and weekend activities. Not all of these activities are purely social: often children are effectively prevented from taking part in extra-mural school activities. Considerable concern was expressed in the UEA survey that many children of secondary school age simply could not stay at school for evening activities or go in at weekends for sporting or cultural events.

It is certainly too easy for urban dwellers to see the rural environment as being ideal for children. One mother, in the Brown and Winyard survey (1975), remarked:

I feel sorry for Jane. She has no one to play with at all. It was affecting her and I felt bound to take her to a playgroup which is twelve miles away. I drive there twice a week though we can't really afford it. The children are never able to go swimming or to music lessons or anything like that. Its bad enough now but it will get worse as they grow older.

Another mother agreed:

It's the children that lose out — they can't go anywhere. There is a Youth Club run by the school and although my husband tries to take them once a week, he can't guarantee to be free to do so. In any case we can't always afford the petrol.

3 HOUSEWIVES

In the UEA study, only 31 per cent of the economically inactive women interviewed nearly always had a car available for their use: over half did not in any case have a driving licence. And Hillman *et al.* (1976) found that amongst 'young women' living in surveyed villages in the Outer Metropolitan Area, 88 per cent had a car in the household — but only 44 per cent also had a licence and optional use of the car.

Rural women, with children and without a car, have real problems as some of the preceding quotations suggest. One particular problem derives from the burden of accompanying children to and from school, sometimes four times a day. This can eat into the amount of time available for other things and if the bus services are not favourably timed, shopping trips to town can be ruled out by this fact alone (see figure 4.6). The UEA study revealed two particular trips which posed problems for the carless mother — trips to the doctor both for herself and for her children, and trips to shops outside the village. In addition many respondents referred to the impossibility of taking up part-time employment, even if a suitable job could be found. And it must always be remembered that young mothers need mobility as much for their own social and psychological well-being as to fulfil their maternal role: feelings of boredom, loneliness and isolation are often serious problems amongst mothers living in rural areas away from the formal and informal networks of support found in towns.

Conclusion

It is clear that rising prosperity and a substantial increase in car ownership in rural areas have not solved mobility and accessibility problems found there. Indeed, they have exacerbated them for certain groups in the community. These groups must be identified and made the focus of policy. Certainly an area focus is insufficient: very marked disparities exist cheek by jowl in the same villages. Nor even is a household focus adequate: the family as a unit has few travel needs and the circumstances of its members can also differ considerably. The 'planner' (an aggregate term to include a broad spectrum of rural decision-makers) must pay particular attention to those groups most disadvantaged in mobility terms by the trends we have witnessed and least able to counter that disadvantage by moving house or by gaining use of a car.

What is needed is a disaggregation of the rural accessibility problem into comprehensible 'sub-problems' upon which attention can be focused. The best way to do this is to consider the carless population in terms of relatively homogeneous groups — for example the elderly, housewives, children — and, similarly, to consider separately the various activities to which access is required. The problem then breaks down into the 'elderly people getting to the post office' problem or the 'young people getting to the youth club' problem. Viewed in this way, priorities can be established, policies devised and, most important, progress — or the lack of progress — towards explicit socially based objectives can be measured. This approach is developed in subsequent chapters.

4
Accessibility:
a concept and a tool

The previous chapter described some of the mobility and accessibility problems that many rural residents experience. And chapter 2 suggested that many relevant trends in rural areas are working against the 'natural' alleviation of these problems: gross social disparities in accessibility are likely to persist and perhaps worsen. Some policy initiatives are clearly called for, and the various possibilities are discussed in subsequent chapters. But how are policy initiatives to be fashioned and evaluated in the context of specific rural areas? The purpose of the present chapter is to argue that the concept of accessibility, suitably developed and given operational form, provides the basis for answering that question. Thus, it seeks to provide a more rigorous conceptual framework for considering the problems of mobility and accessibility in rural areas and it concludes by outlining one practical way of measuring accessibility which could prove widely applicable in rural planning.

What is required of our analytical tool? Essentially it should provide an objective means of assessing the performance of a given 'system' (involving transport and land-use elements) in terms of the alleviation of defined problems of personal accessibility. In doing this, it should indirectly benefit the process of *generating* alternative systems, which would be developed with an eye to their likely alleviation of those problems. The need is for sound and useful operational indices which would make clear who is benefiting (and losing) from alternative policies. I would, therefore, agree with Briggs and Jones who, having reviewed the deficiencies of conventional land-use transportation planning, concluded that to measure the performance of a transport plan by reference to a quantitive measure of the level of mobility conferred by that mix and geographical configuration of transport facilities for discrete groups of the population would clearly show the decision-makers (and the population being planned) precisely who was benefiting from the improvements and by how much. (Briggs and Jones, 1973, p.13)

(The present author would replace 'mobility' in the above statement by 'accessibility': see pp.56-8 for a discussion of these terms.) Such an approach would in effect link rural transport and land-use planning closely to social policy in that the planner's concern would be to modify and monitor certain measures of social well-being and progress — in this case, those associated with personal accessibility to different opportunities.

Some deficiencies of conventional transport planning

The conventional land-use transportation planning process, as used and developed in studies of major urban areas, has not apparently been applied to an essentially rural area. Nevertheless, a brief consideration of certain of the characteristics of that process may be useful in making clear why it seems less useful for the planner to model *actual* trip-making than to concentrate on the opportunities that rural residents enjoy — why, in fact, conventional transport modelling has little to offer in the rural context.

It is not intended to review here the various stages of the conventional land-use transportation modelling process (trip-generation, modal split, traffic assignment, etc.). Suffice it to say that the 'whole process is centred around a concept of attempting to produce a plan for transportation that will satisfy a particular demand. It is assumed that this demand may be predicted accurately and it is assumed that the desirable end-product is to meet that predicted demand' (Stopher and Mayburg, 1975, p.220). Just why such studies should have this central concern and should make these assumptions need not concern us here. (They derive in part from the typical context in which the studies were undertaken in the 1960s and early 1970s — large, rapidly changing urban areas; a central concern for rising car ownership; an expectation of large investment funds for new and modified infrastructures; a belief that society should cater for all of the demand for mobility which was anticipated by a future date.) The point is that the two assumptions mentioned by Stopher and Mayburg (that demand may be accurately predicted and that meeting that demand is in itself the desirable end-product) now seem highly questionable — particularly in a rural context.

The problem is that conventional transport models rely on the actual use of transportation as evidence of 'demand'. The model builders derive statistical relationships between actual use and certain attributes of the households under consideration, and then estimate *future* trip-rates using the statistical relationship, having estimated the magnitude of the various attributes for some future date. Unfortunately, in the rural context (and quite probably in the urban context too) it is unrealistic to assume that the total number of trips made by a household is independent of the quality of transport provision available to that household. As Plowden has observed:

> how many trips people make, where, when and how they make them are obviously all affected by the availability, quality and price of the transport facilities available and also by the location and quality of the facilities which satisfy different journey purposes. These considerations are entirely neglected in trip generation and inadequately represented in later stages. (Plowden, 1974, p.3)

To ignore this reality is to confuse 'demand' with 'supply'. Indeed the whole essence of the 'rural transport problem' is that many strongly felt desires for transport are frustrated because of the imperfections of the market — by indivisibilities in the public supply of transport, institutional inadequacies, lack of market research by the operators, etc. Thus to model the existing pattern of movement as a basis for estimating a future pattern of demand which should be catered for, is *to assume the rural transport problem out of existence.*

And so, a major criticism of the possible application of conventional transport models in a rural context concerns their assumptions about the *non-users* of the transport facilities available. The conventional models ignore such people (except as sufferers of externalities such as noise pollution). Yet often it is the non-users who are the principle sufferers of accessibility-related problems. They may be non-users because the household car has already been pre-empted by the 'head of household' or because they are too young or too old to drive, or because there is simply no public or private transport available to them. Whatever the explanation, their immobility should be a focus of concern, not a reason for their being ignored.

Thus, in using present-day behaviour as indicative of an acceptable balance between the supply of and demand for transport facilities — a balance which can then be used as the basis for predicting future deficiencies in transport supply — the planner is totally ignoring present-day problems. His concern is to avoid hypothetical *future* problems. 'Transportation studies are at fault in concentrating all their attention on future problems and in assuming away present problems, and it is difficult to see how their predictive methods can be altered to take account of the fact that the present cannot be used as a model of the future' (Plowden, 1974, p.8). As Stopher and Mayburg (1975, p.220) put it 'there is no acknowledgement . . . that a preferable way of proceeding may be to attempt to specify an end-state or set of goals and determine the way in which these goals might be met.' This shift to an explicit focus on problems, today's problems, is an important prerequisite of effective rural accessibility planning.

Related to these points of criticism concerning the potential application of conventional transport models in a rural context, is the way they typically measure the quality of transport systems. Generally they subsume measures of the difficulty or unpleasantness of making trips into a generalized cost function which includes (in the case of public transport) the fare paid, the time spent walking to and from the route, time spent waiting and travelling, etc. Their concern is with the ease and the cost of travel, with total trip duration playing a very important role. But in the rural context the duration of the trip (and, as a corollary, the amount of time saved by alternative policies) is a relatively small consideration: much more important is whether the trip is possible at all! Thus, the focus in evaluation has to shift to the existence, frequency and timing of transport services and to whether, in the context of the location and 'opening hours' of different services or activities, these combine to permit or to frustrate a desired trip.

There are other fundamental criticisms that could be made of conventional transport models as they might be applied in rural areas — for example, criticisms relating to their typical lack of consideration of policies relating to the alternative location and opening hours of desired activities, or to the conservatism with which they accept the present-day institutional context and operating structures. Later chapters will emphasize the important of removing these particular sets of blinkers before real improvements can be made in rural accessibility. But the essential point has already been made above: the urgent need in rural areas is for a clear *problem* focus, and this conventional transport models patently lack.

Something of very great importance to the formulation and evaluation of rural accessibility policies follows from this realization that today's pattern of travel is so constrained by the supply situation as to tell us very little. It is that the central focus of concern must be *opportunities*, not behaviour. Actual behaviour is just one sub-set of 'possible behaviours' and it is with the inequalities and determinants of the latter that the rural accessibility planner should primarily be concerned. This conclusion quickly takes us to the concept of 'accessibility' and to its central role in any evaluation of rural transport and location policies.

Accessibility

'Accessibility is . . . a slippery notion . . . one of those common terms that everyone uses until faced with the problem of defining and measuring it' (Gould, 1969, p.64). When we talk about something being 'accessible' we are referring, to put it crudely, to the degree to which it is 'get-at-able'. But the reasons why someone or something may be 'inaccessible' or 'difficult to get at' may be quite varied. An aloof boss may be located in the next room and yet be inaccessible because of the bureaucratic paraphernalia with which he surrounds himself. A well-paid job, a pretty girl or a desirable residence may each be located only five minutes away and yet be effectively inaccessible because one's inadequate skills, social talents or income effectively place them out of bounds! But these *social* dimensions of accessibility are not the concern of this book. We are concerned instead with the inaccessibility of rural residents which arises from their being physically or spatially separated from the thing desired. Hagerstrand (1974, p.5) put it this way:

> Accessibility has at least two sides. One is legal/social. Frequently an individual must fulfil certain requirements in terms of training, age, ability to pay, support from others and so on in order to be permitted to pass the barrier around the supply point he wants to reach. The other is the physical. He must be able to command the transportation facilities which are needed for reaching the supply points at suitable times.

But this distinction is not to deny the existence of important inter-relationships between the two concepts. For example, an improvement in a person's physical access to alternative places of work may bring social and economic benefits which could increase the 'social accessibility' that he or she enjoys.

Concerning *physical* accessibility there is a good deal of common ground in the following definitions: 'the ease with which people can reach distant but necessary services' (Daly, 1975, p.75); 'the ability of people to reach destinations at which they can carry out a given activity' (Mitchell and Town, 1976, p.3) and 'the inherent characteristic, or advantage, of a place with respect to overcoming some form of spatially operating source of friction, for example time and/or distance' (Ingram, 1971, p.101). Each takes as central the capacity to overcome space (hence the words 'ease', 'ability to reach', 'overcoming friction'). But Ingram's definition usefully introduces two sources of disagreement which are of major importance.

First, is the concept of accessibility divorced from the nature of the desired destination? Ingram implies that it is, but each of the other authors include within their definitions a reference to the destination — hence 'necessary services' (Daly) and 'given activity' (Mitchell and Town). In line with the latter authors, we would argue that in *his* definition Ingram is excessively concerned with *mobility* (rather than accessibility). Mobility relates simply to people's *ability to move*. It depends upon such things as the person's physical attributes and disabilities, his monetary resources, the availability of mechanized means of transport and of appropriate infrastructure, but *not* upon the opportunities which may or may not present themselves as a result of his moving. Accessibility alone incorporates this latter feature. A related point is that increasing mobility alone need contribute little to a person's quality of life, since travel is rarely an end in itself. But improving accessibility to employment opportunities, to medical care or to less tangible things such as a varied and novel range of experiences — this is much more closely linked to the quality of life as it is normally understood and is therefore a more valuable objective for the planning process.

Second, who or what experiences accessibility? In the three definitions above, Ingram refers to 'places', the other authors to 'people'. Geographers, the main students of accessibility, have almost all agreed with Ingram — they have sought to define and portray the *spatial* pattern of accessibility. And yet the key point of the previous chapter, which was concerned with the accessibility problems experienced in rural areas, was that in any given place the circumstances of different people may be vastly different. To say that a certain village enjoys a certain level of accessibility is to summarize much too crudely the position of the middle-class woman in a two-car household and the elderly person without a car. They may be neighbours but they live in different worlds and our measure of accessibility, to be useful, should reflect this. To recap, it is the spatial dimension of access- ibility with which we are concerned, but the 'score-sheet' that we use should have social dimensions. Nevertheless, before proceed- ing, it may be useful to look first at some attempts to calculate levels of accessibility using a spatial score-sheet.

Some approaches to measuring accessibility

Measures of accessibility, then, incorporate two elements — *units of separation* between the person or place in question and his destination, and *a measure of the utility of the various destinations*. Often, as stated above, such measures have been primarily place- based and in this case the ultimate purpose has often been to establish a correlation between the measured accessibility of the place and other of its socio-economic characteristics such as its history of population growth or its social well-being. But if the purpose instead is to derive a tool which can be used for evaluating alternative transport and locational policies, it may be as useful to derive *comparative* measures of accessibility (which trade-off units of separation against the number of destinations which become accessible) as to use such *composite* measures (which *combine* the two factors into a single index). Each warrants discussion.

COMPOSITE MEASURES

The most well-known kind of composite accessibility measure is, of course, the index of 'population potential', based upon the

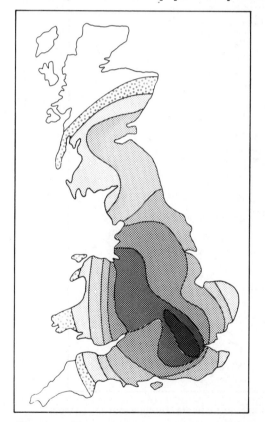

Figure 4.1 The 'population potential' of Great Britain (dark shading denotes high 'potential': see text) (after Clark, 1966)

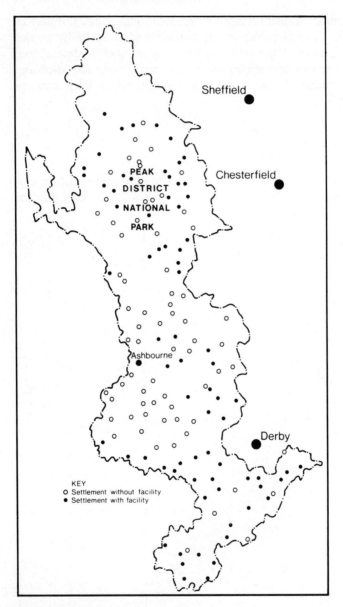

Figure 4.2 West Derbyshire: settlements having a journey to work
service to and from a major urban centre
Source: Derbyshire County Council (1975)

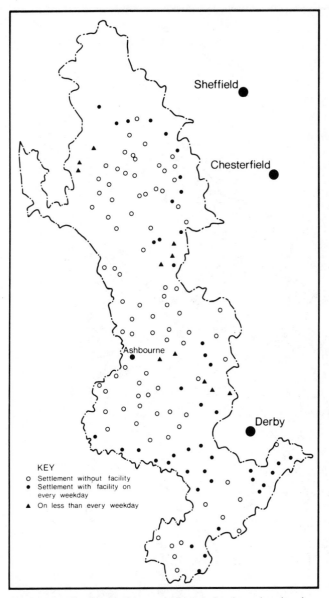

KEY
○ Settlement without facility
● Settlement with facility on
every weekday
▲ On less than every weekday

Figure 4.3 West Derbyshire: settlements having a bus leaving
an entertainment centre after 10 pm
Source: Derbyshire County Council (1975)

61

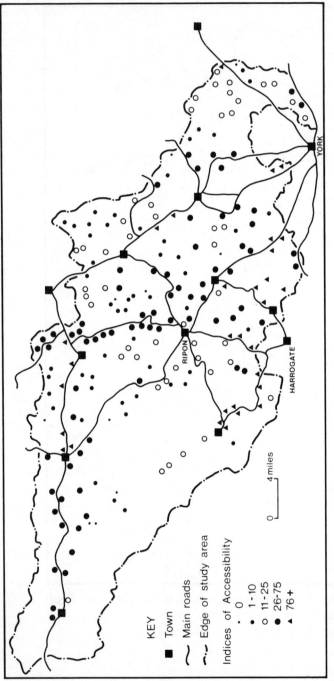

KEY

■ Town
⌒ Main roads
⌒ Edge of study area

Indices of Accessibility

· 0
○ 1-10
◌ 11-25
● 26-75
▲ 76+

Figure 4.4 Indices of accessibility of villages in part of Yorkshire
Source: Johnston (1966)

gravity model. In this, a place's accessibility is a function of its proximity (measured in time, distance or generalized cost for example) to alternative destinations of varying utility. Figure 4.1, for example, shows the 'population potential' of Great Britain. It is effectively a map of 'nearness to other people', but other measures of the utility of destinations could easily be used, for example not 'other people' but 'jobs' or 'retail floorspace'.

Another simple approach is to categorize our spatial units, villages for example, in terms of the quality of the links they enjoy to specified destinations. There are countless examples of this in the literature, but two maps taken from a study of western Derbyshire (Derbyshire County Council, 1975) illustrate the point. These show those villages in the area which have public transport services suitable for work trips to a major employment centre (figure 4.2) or for leisure trips home from an entertainment centre (figure 4.3). It is a simple matter to go on to produce some composite index, in effect superimposing a whole range of such maps, as in Johnston's work (1966) on North Yorkshire. In that study the author awarded points to settlements according to whether they had a daily bus service arriving in a town before 8 a.m. (two points), a Sunday service (one point), etc. and then plotted the resultant indices as a map of accessibility by public transport (figure 4.4.). Clearly approaches such as these are crude, but they could be developed by a more careful, 'market research' based assessment of the services that people consider to be important and the degree to which they would themselves weight their importance.

COMPARATIVE MEASURES

Comparative measures of accessibility indicate the number of opportunities that become accessible as more and more distance is traversed.

The following diagram illustrates the opportunities accessible to residents:

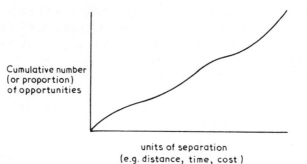

In its simplest form this 'model' would relate to the access enjoyed by residents of a single place, but it could easily be adapted to portray the mean level of access enjoyed by the residents of *all* of the places in a spatial system. Another useful development would be to modify it to show access by the members of a single group (e.g., young mothers) to the opportunities of activities relevant to them, or access by a certain mode (e.g., public transport). An urban example of this approach is provided by the work of Wachs and Kumagai (1972). They

Table 4.1 *Access to health care facilities, Los Angeles 1970*

Facilities	South central		Bell Gardens	
	by car	by public transport	by car	by public transport
No. of health care opportunities *within 15 minutes* travel time:				
General practitioners	335	11	285	18
Hospitals and clinics	40	2	41	0
Total	375	13	326	18
No. of health care opportunities *within 30 minutes* travel time:				
General practitioners	1534	112	1529	36
Hospitals and clinics	143	14	149	1
Total	1677	126	1678	37

Source: Wachs and Kumagai (1972)

looked at four groups of people in Los Angeles (those living in the south-central district and in Bell Gardens, with and without a car), and ascertained how many doctors, hospitals and clinics they could effectively get to within 15 minutes and within 30 minutes. Their results (table 4.1) show the very much greater levels of accessibility enjoyed by motorists, but it is the method of study which interests us here: it has not apparently been applied in the British rural context.

Breheny (1974) developed a series of accessibility indicators along these lines. But his preferred method was slightly different in that he took as fixed a given number of opportunities (e.g. 50 per cent of the area's employment opportunities) and sought to define the varying proportion of people who could reach this target number of opportunities within increasing time or distance bands. Thus:

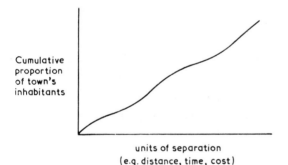

units of separation
(e.g. distance, time, cost)

An actual application of this approach, again taking a study of an American city, is that of Sherman *et al.* (1974) who established the cumulative proportion of suburban Boston's residential zones which enjoyed access to a single major employment centre in the city, as travel time increased. Figure 4.5 portrays their findings, for both car and public transport modes.

Each of the various measures described above has strengths and

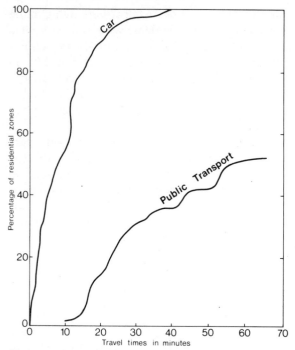

Figure 4.5 Accessibility to a single major employment centre from residential zones in suburban Boston 1970
Source: Sherman *et al.* (1974)

weaknesses. The main point being argued at this stage is that *some sort* of accessibility measuring exercise, respecting the circumstances of different sorts of people, should provide the basis of any evaluation of alternative transport and land-use plans for rural areas. (Mitchell and Town, 1976, provide a good recent review of socially relevant accessibility measures.)

Time-geography

The case for using a measure or measures of accessibility in the evaluation of alternative strategies is strengthened if one considers the work of the Swedish school of 'time-geography' pioneered by Hagerstrand (1970; 1973; 1974) and his disciples (Carlstein, 1975; Martensson, 1975). In common with other commentators Hagerstrand has stressed that evaluation should rest on measuring *opportunities* rather than predicted behaviour, making virtually the same point as that made above in the critique of conventional models:

> the trouble with the behavioural approach is that people rather easily adjust to conditions except when situations cause extreme tensions. One cannot therefore know for certain which parts of the shown behaviour are enforced by circumstances and adopted as acceptable and which express preferences which would come out freely in a set of options without narrow barriers. (Hagerstrand, 1974, p.12)

His point is that evaluation should rest not on what people do or are likely to do, but on what they are able to do. And he argues that the perspective should be that of the single individual. What is his or her 'action space'? What determines its dimensions? What can be done to expand it, or to put more opportunities within its bounds?

These questions are best explored with the aid of a diagram (figure 4.6) which portrays geographic space on the horizontal plane and time on the vertical axis. In the example given, attention is focused on the 24-hour day of a hypothetical mother living in village A, a few miles from a small town. For certain periods of the day she is confined to her home — namely until 09.15 by sleep and family commitments, from 12.00-13.00 which is the family lunchtime, from 16.00-18.00 when she welcomes the children from school and prepares the tea, and after 22.00 when she again prepares for bed. Outside those hours when she is normally confined to her home, the distance over which the woman can travel is dictated by the availability of transport. We assume, in the example, that the household car is used by the husband except in the evening, that the woman can bicycle and that there is a once-daily bus service into town.

Thus in the morning she is able to travel by bus to the small town where she can spend about an hour shopping before the bus departs and returns her to her village. Note, in the hypothetical example, the very convenient timings of the bus service, given her home commitments, and note also that the speed of the bus dictates the slope of the line between village A and the town. It would not be possible for her to travel equally far in a westward

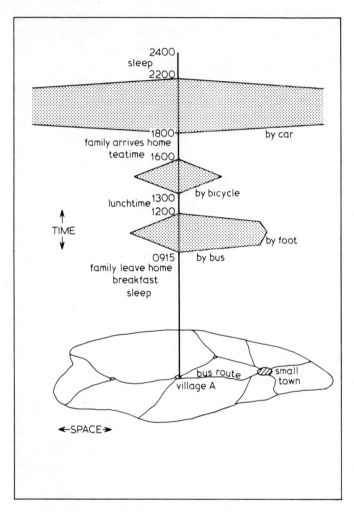

Figure 4.6 The time-space realm of a rural housewife.

direction, but she could, if she wished, go a short distance in that direction by bicycle. In the afternoon she is confined within the distance that she can bicycle, but in the evening she can travel much further afield using the household car.

This simple example illustrates a number of important principles. The woman is subject to two important sets of constraints. First are those relating to herself, in particular her inability to be in two places at once (as an individual she is, literally, indivisible) and her time-commitments. Second are those relating to her environment: here we include not only the technology and availability of the means of transport (the word 'availability' subsuming routeing, timing, and cost) but also two characteristics of the activities to which she seeks access — namely their location and their temporal availability. Clearly if the small town shops which we assume her to visit in the morning were instead located an equal distance to the *west* of village A, or were open not in the morning but in the afternoon, then as far as the woman is concerned they might just as well not exist. As Hagerstrand puts it, we are all the prisoners of 'space-time prisms' (the woman's 'space-time prism' being indicated by the shaded area of figure 4.6). The challenge of rural accessibility planning is to enlarge those prisms, or else to make more activities available within them. This statement provides a lead into the policy options which are briefly listed at the end of the present chapter.

The reader is referred to the Swedish literature cited in this section for a fuller discussion of 'time geography' and of its rich potential as a tool for evaluating rural land-use and transport policies. A computer based application of the model in rural Sweden is reported briefly in English in Martensson (1975). She establishes the varying levels of accessibility enjoyed by different rural places and groups of people, given their transport and land-use environment in its spatial and temporal dimensions.

Measuring accessibility in rural Norfolk

Building upon these notions of time-geography, the UEA research team developed and applied a simple technique for measuring accessibility within parts of rural Norfolk. This may usefully be summarized here, but for a fuller discussion see Moseley *et al.* (1977). Attention was directed to two study areas, each of about 100 square miles and containing about 9000 people. A number of alternative strategies were developed for these areas and the evaluation task was to compare them with one another and with the existing situation, in terms of the benefits of accessibility that they afforded. (The costs that each strategy imposed upon the public sector were separately evaluated, but that exercise is not reported here.)

The basic idea was to focus upon 'group/activity' combinations, for example 'retired people/post office', or 'teenagers/extra-mural education'. The central question asked with respect to each strategy concerned how far it permitted groups of carless people to reach specified activities, without an 'unreasonable' amount of inconvenience. In effect, the task was to write 'yes' or 'no' in each of the cells of a matrix like the one set out below, with regard to each of a large number of constituent villages or zones, and to each strategy in turn.

	ACCESS TO:	chemist	food-shop	post office	pub	etc.
	BY:					
SOCIAL GROUPS	elderly					
	housewives					
	economically active males, etc.					

These answers were then summed in three ways so as to bring out the relevant dimensions of accessibility — namely the spatial dimension (are the residents of place A better served than those of place B?), the activity dimension (is access to chemists greater than access to foodshops?) and, most important, the social dimension (are retired people, as a group, as well served as housewives?) The approach was, in effect, a variant of the 'goals achievement matrix' first developed by Hill (1968) and subsequently described by Lichfield et al. (1975) with each goal relating to accessibility and being expressed in 'group/activity' terms.

In practice the UEA research team considered five 'social groups', namely economically active males, economically active females working full-time or working part-time, economically inactive females under the age of retirement (in effect, 'housewives') and retired people of either sex. An important distinction was drawn between those with and those without ready use of a car. In other words, the definition of groups was based on considerations of life-cycle, economic role and car availability. Twenty-five specific 'activities' were considered, falling into six basic categories — employment, shopping, health, finance, administration and leisure. And in each of the two study areas in Norfolk attention was directed to the circumstances of about 50 villages or small zones.

The various alternative strategies comprised statements of the spatial distribution of people and of activities and of the public transport network, with precise bus and rail timetables and the times of availability of the various activities being carefully specified. Whether these strategies were deemed to be successful in ensuring access to the various activities for the groups in question, was in practice determined with reference to a number of 'reasonable standards' relating to acceptable waiting time, journey time, walking distance, frequency per week, etc. These 'standards' were based on crude empirical evidence and varied between groups and between activities.

The whole research exercise was performed manually, though it could conceivably have been computerized. Figures 4.7, 4.8 and 4.9 portray *one* of the strategies, termed Strategy One or 'S 1', developed for one of the areas — the North Walsham area of Norfolk. Figures 4.10 and 4.11 set out graphically some of the output of the accessibility analyses of this and a number of alternative strategies, the former giving an 'inter-activity' comparison, and the latter an 'inter-group' comparison. It is not intended here to discuss what these analyses actually revealed but a few points will be made about the usefulness of the method.

The central point is that it measures the *opportunity* that alternative strategies afford, not the degree to which systems are actually *used*: this follows from the argument propounded earlier in this chapter. Second, it is susceptible to the explicit weighting of the importance of different components — these are implicitly considered to be of equal importance in the exercise described. For example, if it were considered that the accessibility needs of the elderly are twice as important as those of economically active males, or that access to doctors is twice as important as access to pubs, then this weighting could be incorporated. Third, any fixed route, fixed-time transport service could be incorporated into the analysis — for example school-buses, 'works buses' and post-buses as well as conventional stage services. But unpredictable services,

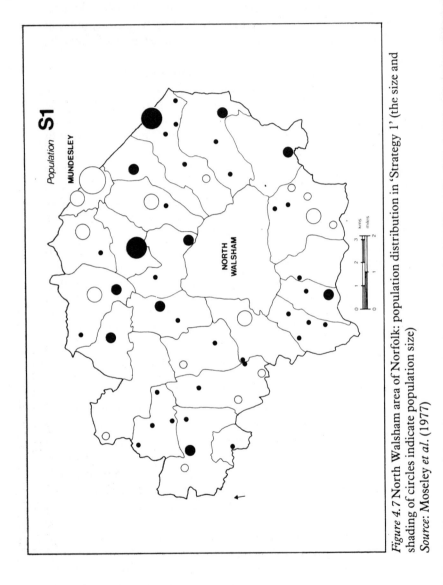

Figure 4.7 North Walsham area of Norfolk: population distribution in 'Strategy 1' (the size and shading of circles indicate population size)

Source: Moseley *et al.* (1977)

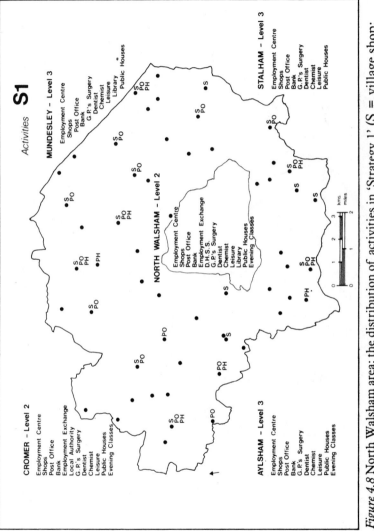

Figure 4.8 North Walsham area: the distribution of activities in 'Strategy 1' (S = village shop; PO = post office; PH = public house)
Source: Moseley *et al.* (1977)

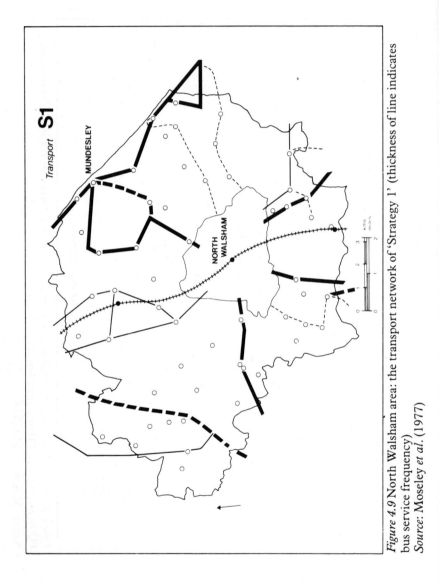

Figure 4.9 North Walsham area: the transport network of 'Strategy 1' (thickness of line indicates bus service frequency)
Source: Moseley *et al.* (1977)

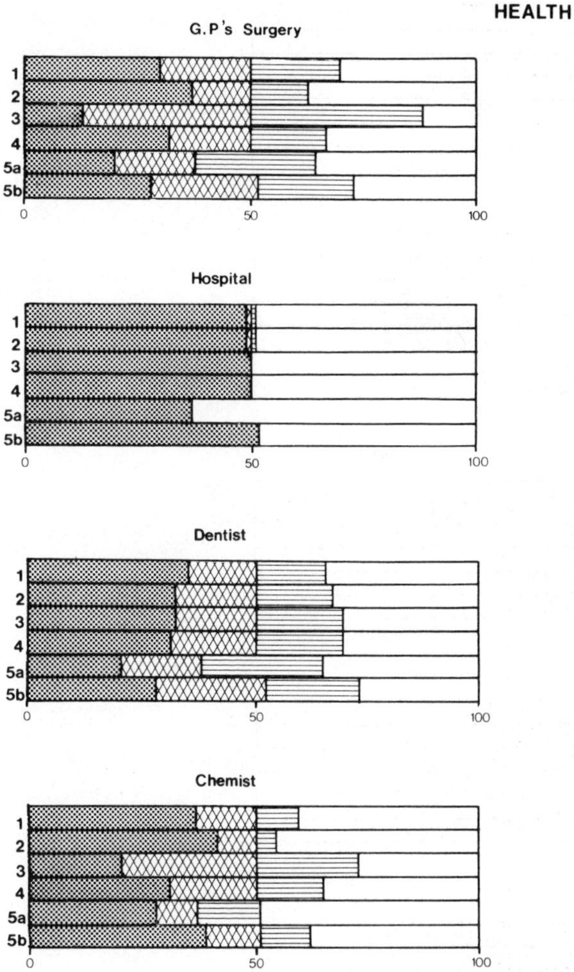

Figure 4.10 North Walsham area: six strategies compared in terms of the access they offered to health activities. (Note: the six strategies are numbered 1,2 . . . 5b. The horizontal axis relates to the proportion of resident population. The key to the shading is:
white: access only by car
horizontal lines: by car and by public transport
crossed lines: by public transport or by foot
stippled: access impossible)
Source: Moseley *et al.* (1977)

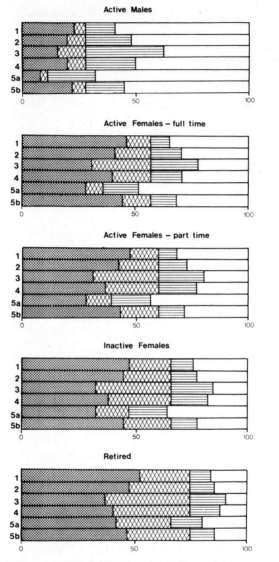

Figure 4.11 North Walsham area: six strategies compared in terms of the access they afford to different social groups
(see figure 4.10 for note and source).

without precise timetables, cannot easily be accommodated. It would be wrong to devote too much space to a discussion of this one technique — it has various deficiencies which are discussed in the research team's report. But it *does* respect the fundamental requirements of the planning process in that it provides a framework for the explicit evaluation in welfare terms of a wide range of alternative policies. In that sense it provides a simple basis upon which better evaluation methodologies might build.

Conclusion

This chapter has stressed the very limited potential value in a rural context of conventional modelling procedures. An emphasis upon opportunities is likely to be much more valuable than one on behaviour. The evaluative tool should be problem-based — in terms of the opportunities which at present tend to be denied to many people — rather than based upon estimates of notional travel demand. It should also respect and reflect the heterogeneity of society.

This is not to say, of course, that calculating measures of accessibility should comprise the whole evaluation exercise. Obviously, careful attention needs also to be directed to the costs incurred in providing the various services, and in order to arrive at the costs of service provision net of revenue, patronage and therefore likely behaviour must be estimated. Equally, attention must be directed to externalities such as the effects that, say, re-routeing a bus service or closing a village school might have upon community life: accessibility is not the sole consideration even within the social domain.

But nevertheless accessibility, as discussed in this chapter, *is* potentially a very useful concept for practical rural planning. Indeed, it may be useful to conclude this chapter, and to link it with later chapters which set out the range of policy options, by referring again to the 'space-time prism' of a hypothetical rural resident (figure 4.6). That diagram suggests six ways of improving the woman's accessibility:

(i) *mobility*
    (a) facilitate her ability to travel from village A to the small town and to other useful destinations;

(b) establish mobile services going out from the small town, or from other places, to village A;

(ii) *location*

(a) locate more activities within the woman's 'action space' (e.g., a branch library at village A);

(b) persuade the woman to move to an alternative residence in the small town;

(iii) *time*

(a) reduce the constraints impinging on the woman's time-budget (i.e., reduce or rearrange the black portions on the time axis);

(b) increase or modify the opening hours of the activities (e.g., encourage shopkeepers to open in the evenings occasionally, when she has a car available).

Any of these six options would increase the person's accessibility: they form the basis of chapters 6 and 7.

5
Powers, responsibilities and resources

The nature of the 'rural accessibility problem' has now been described and we have briefly examined just what is meant by that central but elusive objective 'accessibility'. But how is that problem to be alleviated and that objective to be better attained? The answer to this question lies not just in a consideration of the range of policy options, although that will be the concern of chapters 6 and 7. It rests also on the legal, administrative and financial context within which relevant decisions are taken. It is this context which provides the substance of the present chapter, which falls into three major parts. First is a brief historical review of the major items of legislation and of associated policy developments. Second is an examination of the mass of public agencies which are involved in some way in rural accessibility and a consideration of the ways in which they interact, or fail to interact. Third is a review of the financial resources available or potentially available for the alleviation of rural inaccessibility.

Powers and policies: the historical dimension

Obviously it is impossible in a few paragraphs to describe all the items of legislation or of government policy which have affected the levels of access that rural residents presently enjoy. Earlier chapters, in demonstrating the breadth of the accessibility issue and of the various forces which impinge upon it, have in effect already ruled out so comprehensive an objective. All that is possible here is to itemize four or five major pieces of legislation and to suggest how policies in other fields might also have had an impact. Consideration of the 1978 Transport Bill (not yet law, at the time of writing) is deferred until chapter 8.

The Road Traffic Act of 1930 (amended in 1960) is of major importance as it introduced the road service licensing system which remains substantially in force today. Designed originally to introduce an element of stability in a climate of ruthless competition and instability, it continues uneasily in the totally different climate of rural Britain today. The operation of the road service licensing system is discussed in some detail below when we consider the Traffic Commissioners whose job it is to operate it, but the point here is that the Road Traffic Acts may have helped to make more orderly the retreat of the rural bus operator, but they have been quite unable to avert it. Once the forced cross subsidy of unremunerative rural services from the proceeds of their once profitable urban counterparts became no longer possible, then the Traffic Commissioners were forced into restricting their attention to the *details* of rural bus services rather than to their overall *scale*. Indeed some would argue that the heavy hand of regulation has in fact hindered the development of alternative, innovative, forms of rural transport. This debate must be returned to: chapter 6 refers to legislation introduced in 1977 to allow the localized and short-term relaxation of road service licensing for experimental purposes, and the 1978 Transport Bill (chapter 8) promises further reforms relating to small vehicles. Suffice it to say now that the process of bus service regulation, designed to protect the public by protecting the bona fide bus operator, is a contentious but important part of the backcloth against which new policy developments must be assessed.

A second major piece of legislation which has radically affected the accessibility that rural residents enjoy is the 1944 Education Act. Not only did the Act impose upon local authorities the responsibility of preparing development plans for education, showing where schools were to be built, expanded or closed, but it also introduced the principle that in certain circumstances the cost of a pupil's travel to school should be borne by the state. Essentially, the local education authority must ensure the provision of, and pay for, adequate transport for all children living more than three miles from school (two miles in the case of children under 8 years). Discretionary powers allow the local authority to do likewise for shorter trips. Leaving aside the enormous social and educational benefits of such a policy, let us simply note that it has necessarily made all county councils major forces in the transport development of the rural areas of their counties. The Act also marked the introduction of a pioneer 'standard' into rural transport planning ('all children living over three miles from their school shall have free transport as a right') — perhaps a generously high standard of provision which might sit uncomfortably with standards in other fields of rural transport if ever these are developed.

Before considering the next major item of rural transport legislation, the 1968 Transport Act, we must recognize the precursor of its rural transport clauses — the Jack Committee's report on Rural Bus Services (Jack Committee, 1961). This committee was charged with examining the adequacy of rural bus services in England (there were parallel studies in Scotland and Wales) and with advising on methods of ensuring their adequacy in the future. Already rising car ownership was taking its toll and the committee concluded that 'the present and probably future levels of rural bus services are not adequate to avoid a degree of hardship and inconvenience sufficient to call for special steps, and we recommend mainly a system of direct financial assistance, in part from central sources and administered through county councils.' This recommendation, or more strictly this set of three recommendations (direct financial assistance; in part from central sources; administered through county councils), was a major step forward, though it took seven years for it to be embodied in legislation and more than ten years for it to find real expression on the ground.

The 1968 Transport Act re-organized the financing and the control of public transport in Britain. It established the National Bus Company (in Scotland, the analogous Scottish Transport Group) to take over previously nationalized bus companies and some which were in private hands. The NBC has a commercial remit — in short, it has to pay its way — and is a federation of regional bus companies each with a good deal of autonomy. This commercial remit, and the manner of its interpretation on the ground by these regional bus companies, have been major factors in fashioning the rural public transport system of the 1970s.

The 1968 Act also put the county councils firmly on the stage:

previously they had had very little contact with bus operators except in the execution of their responsibilities under the 1944 Education Act and in making objections to the Traffic Commissioners about the operators' proposed fare increases. Section 34 of the Act established the principle that the final decision on whether a rural bus service is or is not essential should lie with the county councils (i.e., not with the operators, nor with central government). For the first time, the county councils were empowered, but not required, to make good the losses incurred by specific rural bus services.

Two other channels for subsidizing the bus industry were also introduced by the 1968 Act: a rebate on fuel tax paid by commercial operators, and the 'new bus grant' which has encouraged operators to improve their vehicle stock. Both of these are central government responsibilities and although until very recently they proved financially more important than the subsidy of specific services by the county councils, it is the latter which is intrinsically more interesting as a tool for 'managing the rural accessibility system' since it lies in local hands and it allows for a good deal of local discrimination and fine tuning.

In practice, the county councils' response to their Section 34 powers was slow in taking shape and extremely variable geographically. Most counties did little or nothing until the 1970-71 avalanche of requests for subsidies came in from new, commercially conscious, NBC subsidiaries. Faced with a demand that they pay up or lose this or that service, some counties opted meekly for the latter alternative. Others met all or nearly all of the requests. Both sympathy for the isolated rural resident and the degree to which the operators' requests were rigorously appraised varied greatly from county to county: rules of thumb proved as common as evaluation techniques which looked carefully at costs and at social objectives (Moyes, 1975). In practice many county councils strove to sustain most existing services while trying to pay the operators a sum approximating to the *marginal* cost of running threatened services, rather than the *average* cost which the operators not unnaturally tended to seek. In short the early 1970s were a period in which both county councils and the operators tentatively felt their way in a new field of responsibility. Figure 5.1 reveals the importance of bus subsidies in one rural county — Cumbria. The present network of services

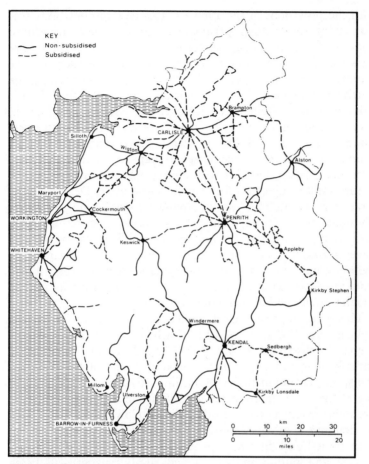

Figure 5.1 Cumbria's scheduled bus network: subsidized and non-subsidized routes in 1976
Source: Cumbria County Planning Department (1976)

would clearly be very much reduced without these payments.

The responsibilities of the local authorities were sharpened in 1974 when the new county and district councils came to power as a result of the 1972 Local Government Act. (Re-organization came a year later in Scotland.) Section 203 of that Act imposed on the new county councils the task of developing 'policies which will promote the provision of a co-ordinated and efficient system of public transport to meet the needs of the county'. Compared with the provisions of the 1968 Act this new responsibility was mandatory rather than permissive, and it at last introduced notions of planning and management in contrast to the *ad hoc* response to subsidy requests which arose from the 1968 Act. To achieve this new managerial role, the county councils were given much-strengthened financial powers (although the Traffic Commissioners retained control over the issue of road service licences and hence over the details of the fares, routes and timings of scheduled bus services). In essence, the county councils are now much freer to spend their own sources of money (from local rates), together with appropriate government grants, as they please, subject to the overall control of the Department of Transport as outlined in the following paragraph. Arbitrary divisions between expenditure on road construction, road maintenance, car parking provision and public transport support have, in principle at least, been swept away: county councils, in their new guise as local transport planners, are very largely free to shift resources within the broad transport umbrella as well as geographically within their counties.

This new approach is embodied in the annual 'Transport Policies and Programmes' (TPPs) which county councils now prepare, subsequent to the 1972 Act. TPPs are intended to embody long-, medium- and short-term views of the counties' transport development, with outline strategies looking 10-15 years ahead, a more detailed 5-year rolling programme of expenditure and a precise costing of the following year's intended programme. Explicit objectives and priorities have to be set out with capital and current expenditure, as well as road and rail, private and public and urban and rural transport, all being brought together in a common planning process. The Department of Transport receives these TPPs each year and uses them as a basis for block payments to the various county councils by means of the Rate Support Grant and the new Transport Supplementary Grant (TSG). The TSG is distributed to local authorities whose estimates of transport expenditure, as expressed in the TPP and accepted by the Department of Transport, exceed a prescribed threshold. The payment of TSG, then, has replaced the previous multiplicity of government grants for specific transport purposes (for example road maintenance, car parking provision and, indeed, rural bus support under the

1968 Transport Act) and has thereby greatly widened the scope for local authorities to develop and implement comprehensive local transport policies.

Despite the mandatory nature of Section 203, however, and despite the impulse towards comprehensive transport planning provided by the TPP system, it seems fair to say that many county councils have not as yet shown any great interest in promoting rural public transport in their counties as distinct from other fields of transport provision. Three reasons may be suggested for this. First, this reluctance doubtless in part derives from the extremely harsh financial climate of the mid-1970s, and county surveyors are quick to point out that other items of rural transport expenditure, notably road maintenance, are both costly and in large part inescapable. Second, the whole ethos and endowment of skills found in the surveyor's/engineer's departments of most shire counties tend to be related more to road building and maintenance and to traffic management rather than to the management of integrated transport systems with social objectives. Third, there is often a certain ideological aversion towards subsidy payments, by the predominantly Conservative controlled councils of the shire counties. (How far *other* items of rural expenditure, for example on postal services or indeed on the maintenance of minor roads, themselves constitute tacit decisions to subsidize, indeed to subsidize the wealthier section of the rural community, is a moot point.)

The development of the legal framework within which decisions affecting rural transport are taken has been outlined at some length above. But, as this is of course the central theme of this book, transport is only one component in the people-link-activity chain which encapsulates 'accessibility'. In that context at least a brief consideration of the spatial planning (sometimes termed 'land-use planning') function of local authorities becomes necessary, although so well covered is this subject in other texts (e.g., Cullingworth, 1976; Hall, 1975) that our review here will be cursory.

The central point is that the county councils have had a spatial planning responsibility for a good deal longer than their transport planning responsibility. The 1947 Town and Country Planning Act imposed on them a duty to prepare county development plans for ministerial approval (then, as now, a different minister unfortunately from the one with responsibility for transport). In these development plans, which were conceived essentially in cartographic rather than written form, virtually all county councils opted for some degree of discrimination between their rural settlements in terms both of service provision — schools, health services, etc. — and of the granting of permissions for residential development. In short, rural spatial planning, as shaped by the various statutes and executed by the county councils, took on three basic functions: to guide public spending agencies in their allocation of resources; to provide a framework for decisions by the private sector; and to channel new residential development to the most suitable places. These basic functions have not changed greatly in recent years although the 1968 and 1971 Town and Country Planning Acts introduced a new system for the preparation of development plans — a system which sees plans more as a process than as an end-state and which separates the development of county-wide strategic principles from the preparation of detailed local plans. The former, termed 'structure' plans, provide (or *will* provide: a large number had still to be submitted or approved in 1978) a basis for the latter and one of the results of local government re-organization has been to transfer responsibility for local planning, and much of the parallel responsibility of 'development control' to new, second-tier, district councils. Few practising planners will argue that this division of responsibility has not been to the detriment of comprehensive spatial planning.

The relevant agencies

'Rural accessibility' is a very broad concept and there is a mass of public bodies or agencies which affect it in one way or another. Consideration of the various roles of these agencies is important for a number of reasons:

(i) no single agency is alone responsible for, or capable of, maintaining adequate levels of accessibility in rural areas, however 'adequacy' might be defined:

(ii) for most relevant agencies accessibility is a secondary consideration if it is a consideration at all: other objectives are usually paramount or better defined;

(iii) in consequence of (i) and (ii), decision-making tends to be fragmented and ill-focused on the accessibility problem;

(iv) while there is no shortage of literature on the powers and policies of individual agencies, how they interact (or fail to interact) one with another has received little attention;

(v) while in the medium or long term a more integrated and purposeful process of accessibility planning and management can and should be developed, in the short run policy measures cannot be more comprehensive or ambitious than the present institutional context allows.

And so, the purpose of the present section is to review the powers, actions and interactions of the principal 'relevant agencies', namely those which affect the location of people or of activities, the transport and communications which link them, and the 'time-budgets' and 'opening hours' which determine whether access is feasible. Inevitably the breadth of this field necessitates a good deal of selectivity. There is also the question of what constitutes 'an agency'. Do local authority social services, planning, and education departments warrant separate attention or should consideration be reserved for the whole legal entity — the county council? The approach to these questions of selection and definition has been a pragmatic one. Agencies have been included if they have a significant effect on the accessibility of rural residents, have their own distinctive set of objectives and powers, and publicly operate as a distinct body or group of bodies. Attention is focused on the situation in England and Wales, though many of the broad conclusions will be applicable elsewhere in the United Kingdom.

1. LOCAL AUTHORITIES

Earlier in this chapter it was shown that the local authorities, particularly the county councils, have a central and increasing role in the field of rural accessibility. To understand that role, and the disappointingly partial way in which it has found expression to date, it is necessary first to appreciate some basic points concerning the nature of their powers, their hierarchical arrangement and their internal fragmentation.

The *powers and responsibilities* of local authorities have evolved

in a very *ad hoc* manner. Initially they took on various local responsibilities such as the upkeep of roads, and they have gradually
taken more upon themselves or been given more responsibilities
by parliament (as noted above). Their powers are of three types:

(a) those associated with *obligatory* functions, for example the
schooling and road maintenance tasks of the county councils;
(b) those associated with *generally permitted* functions, for
example the subsidy of loss-making public transport and the
promotion of industrial development;
(c) those associated with *special legislation*, for example the
operation of bus services, authorized by a private Act of
Parliament.

And so local authorities, compared say, with the West German
Länder whose powers are enshrined in a written federal consti-
tution, are less able to initiate action in new fields, but, as a
corollary, they tend to be more responsible to the initiatives of
central government — a tendency reinforced of course by their
receiving two-thirds of their income from the latter.

It is the variety of ways in which local authorities *interpret* their
powers and responsibilities which is all important in under-
standing their impact upon rural accessibility. Regarding the
three sources of power listed above, there is clearly wide scope for
the use or neglect of the permissive powers but of course there is
also considerable room for alternative interpretations of many of
the obligatory functions. As Dearlove (1973, p.15) put it, quoting
a councillor, 'some law is cut and dried and there is nothing you
can do about it, but there is a lot you *can* do and one can
invariably find a law to enable you to do something if you want
to.' (Perhaps the converse is equally true!)

Eddison (1973) considers local authorities to be positioned
between two ends of a continuum: the 'agency' view of their
powers sees local authorities merely carrying out obligations
imposed by parliament, while the 'initiative' view sees them
going well beyond this to take on a general responsibility for the
well-being of the community. Most authorities lie somewhere
between these two extremes and their varying interpretations of
their rural transport obligations and of the possible value of
adopting a more corporate approach to the policies related to
personal accessibility illustrate this well. This inevitably raises

the issue of the relative merits of, on the one hand, more *mandatory* central government intervention in these fields, or, on the other, greater delegation of responsibility to the local authorities.

Local authorities, of course, exhibit a *hierarchical arrangement*. In the English shire counties the three tiers are the county, district and parish councils. There are sometimes conflicts relevant to rural accessibility (e.g., those arising from differences between county and district councils over the siting of a new shopping development), and in addition the councils nearest to the 'grass roots' tend to have fewer relevant powers and are dependent upon county council action to assuage the criticisms of their constituents. Thus in rural transport, for instance, a district council may find itself in the position of receiving detailed complaints about bus services from individual parish councils, which can only finally be resolved by decisions made by the county council in consultation with nationalized public transport operators.

The third fundamental characteristic of local authorities is their *internal fragmentation*. The actions of local authorities, which affect the accessibility that rural residents enjoy, emanate from a wide range of relatively autonomous departments and associated committees. Many decisions reached in the county planning, social services, education, surveyor's and treasury departments are frequently relevant to rural accessibility but may not be properly coordinated. Similarly, a district council may fail to relate its housing policies to its transport and planning policies.

Many of these points, relating to the powers, hierarchical arrangement and internal fragmentation of local authorities are returned to below in a separate consideration of county, district and parish councils.

(i) County councils

Following the Bains Report (1972) and the 1972 Local Government Act, most of the new county councils established the post of chief executive and organized their chief officers into a management team so as to facilitate the coordination of their activities. Some developed a corporate management approach to their activities or extended such an approach where this already existed. However, many departments in many county councils still tend to function in mutual isolation. Two prime (and related) causes are suggested for this. First, the councils have extensive obligations over a number of important fields and the relevant departments which have emerged are largely concerned with the achievement of aims and standards in one particular field. Second, in order best to achieve the aims of each department, the majority of its staff are specialists in that field at an appropriate level, their training and experience being in the relevant discipline. Because of this, departments tend to work towards the achievement of standards in different aspects of life with little *overall* appreciation of implications for broader issues such as rural accessibility.

For example the *social services department* determines the siting, opening hours and catchment areas of its offices and homes, the provision of specialist transport to day-centres, the degree of any assistance with home telephone installation costs and the provision of certain peripatetic services. The extent of such provision, and the precise siting of such offices, centres and homes, each influence the need for transport provision and the nature of personal problems of accessibility.

Meanwhile the *planning department*, through its structure planning responsibilities and its powers of control over the location of major developments, directly influences the location of people and of activities and the overall pattern of the transport facilities which connect the two. (These spatial planning powers are discussed in greater detail in chapter 7.)

The education department affects rural accessibility in two direct ways. First, it determines the nature and, related to that, the locational pattern of the schooling provided. A decision, for example, to shift from a primary/secondary to a first/middle/high school system implies a good deal both for village development and for transport policy. The Norfolk county council's education plan, approved in 1975, exemplifies this. Its 'middle school' component which involved the channelling of 8-12 year olds to schools in a small number of selected centres directly affected the settlement policy which emerged in the 1977 Structure Plan. This in turn will affect other aspects of the 'rural accessibility system' including the developing pattern of public transport services.

The second direct way in which a county's education department is relevant to these broader considerations concerns its interpretation of the transport responsibilities laid upon it by the 1944 Education Act. It can arrange for public or private operators to provide the necessary transport under contract, it can operate its own fleet of vehicles, or it can underwrite a system whereby school children travel free on stage carriage services. Decisions in this field can have important ramifications. For example, failure to put work out to contract to independent transport operators will reduce the ability of the latter to offer off-peak, marginal cost, services for other users. Similarly, failure to channel school children on to scheduled bus services where the latter exist might result in the eventual withdrawal of those services, or their subsidy by another arm of the county council.

The *surveyor's/transport department* (it is variously called, and in some counties is formally integrated with the planning department) generally has the task of preparing the Transport Policies and Programmes as discussed above, and of carrying out the other transport planning and executive functions given to the county councils in the various pieces of legislation.

Interdepartmental cooperation is not always easy, even if joint committees and working parties exist and even if a Transport Coordinating Officer has been appointed. Often individual departments, not to say chief officers, have their own ethos which other officers find alien or unsympathetic. In this context we can cite a personal communication from a social services officer whose brief was to 'inject a social dimension' into the deliberations leading up to the TPP. He attended the TPP working parties

only occasionally, because notice of meetings is usually very short — i.e., we get the agenda in the morning for a meeting in the afternoon. When we go to the meetings we are usually so overwhelmed with technical data on road building and traffic flows that by the time we get to public transport we're suffering from overkill. In addition I feel uneasy about making comments about the social aspects of public transport when the climate of the meeting is usually hostile and the county surveyor is generally unsympathetic towards our aims.

This simple anecdote may go a long way towards explaining why accessibility planning within most county councils is so fragmented. It certainly seems that despite the comprehensive powers that the 1972 Local Government Act gave to the new county councils in the fields of strategic planning, the provision of social and education services, the coordination of passenger transport and corporate administration, as far as rural accessibility is concerned the problem is one which is the responsibility of most county departments and therefore, in a sense, the responsibility of none.

(ii) *District councils*

Compared with that of the county councils, district council involvement in rural accessibility matters is characterized by less severe problems of coordination, given their smaller geographical area and their more limited responsibilities and powers; closer links with problems felt and expressed at the local scale; and responsibilities which are more permissive than mandatory. In the field of *public transport* some district councils inherited from the old urban district councils the power to operate bus services. However, the regulation of public transport by the Traffic Commissioners has meant that these services tend to remain in the urban parts of the new districts. In addition, district councils have permissive powers to subsidize bus services under Section 34 of the 1968 Transport Act and to promote their own experimental transport schemes. They can also, of course, operate concessionary bus fare schemes and there is great variation between districts in this respect. If their proposed expenditure is approved by the county council it can be included in the TPP submission, but the districts can act independently if they meet the costs themselves.

In general it seems that district councils are better placed to consider truly *local* public transport than counties. They are nearer the 'grass roots' and they also lack the county councils' extensive responsibilities for road maintenance and improvement and the latter's involvement in big city and regional traffic problems. But the district councils' accessibility activities are currently constrained by their lack of a counterpart to the counties' Transport Coordinating Officers, by their duty to work within the framework of county decisions embodied in TPPs and structure plans upon which they have a right only to be consulted and make comments, and by their very limited financial resources with relevant central government transfer payments being directed chiefly to the county councils.

District councils also affect rural accessibility in other important ways, principally in the siting of council housing (for which they have responsibility), in their development control functions, and in the decisions they take concerning the location and 'opening hours' of their various offices.

(iii)   *Parish councils*

Compared with other councils parish councils have very few *executive* powers and these are of a restricted and low cost variety: e.g., the provision of recreation grounds and roadside benches. But parish councils tend to be extremely variable in the extent and character of their actions. Many parishes do not have councils at all. Others, by contrast, are very active both in an executive sense and as a pressure group for change. Often the degree of their activity reflects the size and socio-economic character of the parish. Their most valuable role may well be to serve as a focus for local discussion and as a channel of information and representations to higher tiers of local government and other bodies. They are also strong candidates for organizing 'community self-help' measures, depending on their capacity for action and for being well informed.

2 REGIONAL BODIES

Certain bodies which operate over geographical areas intermediate to the county and the nation hold considerable sway over rural accessibility matters. These bodies are characterized by their specialist role, and by their being ultimately responsible *not* to elected local politicians but to a central government minister with a specific functional concern. The regional subsidiaries of the National Bus Company are discussed, briefly, below. The Regional Water Authorities derive their relevance particularly from their responsibility for sewerage provision and water supply which have very important ramifications in the location of new residential, industrial and service developments. Indeed, often taken without any real consideration of their social implications, decisions on water supply and sewerage generally have major, if indirect and gradual, implications for spatial development and thereby the personal accessibility enjoyed in rural areas.

(i)   *The Regional Health Authorities*

Of the regional bodies, it is valuable to consider in most detail the role of the Regional Health Authority (and its constituent subsidiary agencies) both because of the range of ways in which it affects personal accessibility, and because it exemplifies the problems involved in coordinating 'accessibility decisions' even *within* a single body. The administration and planning of health services within a region are the responsibilities of the three administrative tiers in the re-organized health service. Planning in particular (both short-term operational planning and longer term strategic planning) involves the Regional Health Authority, the Area Health Authority (AHA), the district officers and the various professional representatives in a formal cycle of establishing priorities and guidelines, consultation, plan preparation and approval. The kinds of policies which emerge from this planning process, and the detailed day-to-day management of services affect access to each level of service, from that of the local general practitioner (GP) to the highly specialized services provided by the District General Hospital.

Primary health care   The GP is probably the most commonly encountered representative of the health service, whether in the surgery or in the home. The GP is, however, a contractor and is not employed by the National Health Service, although the Family Practitioner Council (a committee of the AHA) is responsible for administering contracts and paying doctors' salaries. The contractual relationship between the NHS and the GP means that ultimately it is the GP who decides upon such things as surgery hours, the location of surgeries and special transport arrangements for patients, and these matters cannot easily be affected by the NHS planning cycle.

This is important because perhaps the most important trend in primary health care affecting accessibility is the increasing tendency for GPs to work in group practices. It is clear that in rural areas this has resulted in a reduction in the number of 'medical outlets', with some surgeries closing or becoming part-time branches (see chapter 2). This trend towards larger practices has been complemented by the rise of the Primary Health Care Team, in which AHA staff (district or community nurses, midwives and health visitors) are attached to practices.

The rural GP faces particular problems, in that, compared with his urban colleague, he usually has a lower ratio of attendances to home visits, attributable at least in part to poor passenger transport. The point is that it is up to the individual GP to decide how to meet these special problems, and he may operate mobile surgeries, arrange consultations to coincide with the availability of public transport or even provide special transport. Similarly, branch surgeries may be held in temporary accommodation for short periods once or twice per week (at least one such surgery in Norfolk takes place in the local pub). In addition the GP is normally responsible for deciding whether patients can use the hospital car service when referred to out-patient clinics.

Hospital services and management   Decisions to build new hospitals and relocate existing services have obvious effects upon access for employees, visitors and patients. Major decisions are made in accordance with DHSS guidelines, which have, for example, required the concentration of all non-psychiatric in-patient and out-patient services in District General Hospitals. Concern has been expressed about the accessibility problems implied by this (see the discussion in chapter 2) and RHAs and AHAs have since been asked by the DHSS to consider the possible conplementary role of 'community hospitals'. These would be staffed by GPs, would serve catchments of around 50,000 people and would not have in-patients who require specialist treatment. Essentially they would be designed for the chronically sick, geriatrics, and early discharges from the DGHs.

In addition to this strategic issue, a number of day-to-day management decisions, taken by the officers of individual hospitals, affect accessibility — especially in rural areas where those patients, visitors and staff who lack a car have particular problems in travelling to and from the hospital. Some measures which may be taken by the hospital include the following: assisted travel schemes for staff under special circumstances; payment direct to the patient to reimburse travel expenses when the patient would normally need to claim from the Supplementary Benefits Commission; arrangement of out-patient clinics to coincide with bus availability; appointment of officers in the medical records department to coordinate the transport arrangements of patients; the 'unofficial' extension of the normal grounds for providing a hospital car service so as to embrace social reasons; overnight accommodation; arranging special bus services with local operators for staff or patients or augmenting the ambulance service with the use of taxi operators; the provision of residential accommodation for staff.

To conclude, the Regional Health Authorities and their various subsidiary decision-making units affect accessibility by means of a wide range of decisions concerning both the location of their activities and the transport made available to patients, visitors and staff. It appears that often these decisions are so numerous and varied that full coordination is not adequately achieved. It also appears that the health service aptly demonstrates some of the hidden costs of a concentrated spatial distribution of activities, for example those associated with the arrangements listed in the previous paragraph.

3 CENTRAL GOVERNMENT

The role or, to be more accurate, roles of central government in affecting rural accessibility are of major importance, but only a few selected points can be made. Central government involvement derives from three chief sources: first, the financial and regulatory power it wields over more specifically relevant agencies such as British Rail, the NBC, and the local authorities; second, its direct involvement in rural areas through the relevant ministries, as exemplified by the work of the road construction units of the Department of Transport and the operation of job centres by the Department of Employment; third, its fiscal and redistributory policies relating, for example, to the various motoring-related taxes and social security payments.

As far as its direct involvement is concerned, an important feature is the vertical 'chain of command' which tends to typify much government decision-making. Decisions are often taken by separate ministries which, though justified within the immediate field of competence, can upset other fields of activity of which their proponents were unaware. The recent regional strategies mark an attempt to coordinate such decisions at a regional level, but *Strategic choice for East Anglia* (East Anglia Regional Strategy Team, 1974) stressed how much remains to be done in this respect.

The most important single ministries are, of course, the Departments of Environment and Transport. In large part the former's influence is felt via the financial and regulatory powers which it wields over the local authorities. Payment of the rate support grant and the scrutiny of structure plans provide major examples of its influence. The Department of Transport (hived off from DoE in 1976) oversees the nationalized transport undertakings and the Traffic Commissioners, and receives TPPs and determines the allocation of the Transport Supplementary Grant to local authorities. Its potential for improving rural accessibility via these various channels of influence is quite considerable.

Regarding other government departments, there are three basic points that should be made. First, very few of them take *no* decisions bearing upon rural accessibility. For instance, the defence and agriculture ministries are relevant because many of the decisions they take affect rural land-use and the size and socio-economic composition of rural communities. Second, certain public corporations which influence rural accessibility, notably the Post Office Corporation, do not have as a 'parent' government department either Environment or Transport. This supplements any difficulties which arise from conflicts between their briefs as public corporations and their role as contributors to a rural accessibility strategy. Third, certain departments influence rural accessibility directly through the siting, equipping and opening hours of their own rural, or small town 'outlets'. This is true, for example, of the Department of Employment (with its responsibility for paying unemployment benefits, and for assisting with job-seeking and training) and the Department of Health and Social Security. It is noteworthy that rural post offices are important points at which certain pensions may be collected and written information on other benefits obtained, but there is apparently no DHSS involvement in Post Office location policy.

4 PUBLIC CORPORATIONS

A central issue regarding public corporations, and one which is particularly relevant in rural areas, is the perennial conflict between the objectives of profitability and service. A recent newspaper editorial (*The Guardian*, 19 November 1976) aptly commented:

> Clearly the nationalised industries ought not to operate just like private-sector commercially-minded monopolies, but clearly, too, there is a limit to how far they are supposed to pursue the Government's other objectives to buy British, to preserve jobs in development areas, to keep down the price of fuel, to provide transport in rural areas.

This reconciliation is made even more difficult by the unfavourable relationship between the distribution of the *need* for the products of the nationalized industries and that of the *ability to pay* for them. This is true first in the *spatial* dimension (public transport and telephone kiosks may well be of greatest value to people in areas where the net public-sector cost of their supply is greatest) and, second, in the *social* dimension (for example, home telephones are probably most valuable to groups such as the elderly and chronic sick with the lowest purchasing power). Related to this is a point of difference between the various nationalized industries. The electricity authorities and the postal side of the Post Office Corporation are required by statute to provide electricity and mail services to all parts of Britain and can neither refuse to provide nor make exceptional charges. No such limitation is placed on the Gas Corporation, on Post Office telephone operations, or on the transport industries. It would be wrong to argue that such limitations *should* be placed on these latter agencies, but it is clear that this contrast has significant implications for accessibility in rural areas.

Regarding those nationalized transport undertakings with greatest relevance to rural accessibility, notably British Rail and the National Bus Company, there are a number of points that should be made. First, detailed supervision of their operations has become an accepted fact. Their basic brief is to operate commercially but, in the case of British Rail, it is required to run unprofitable services (to fulfil its 'public service obligation') in return for a block payment from central government. (This replaced in 1974 the earlier system whereby the government made specific subsidy payments so that particular passenger services might be continued.) In addition, under the 1972 Local Government Act, non-metropolitan county and district councils can subsidize rail services running wholly or partly within their area. In a similar fashion the local authorities can, if they wish, subsidize NBC bus services, as already discussed.

A second point is that BR and NBC differ in other significant ways, apart from their being subsidized principally by different levels of government. British Rail is run as a single firm and it runs virtually all rail passenger transport in Britain. By contrast the National Bus Company is a holding company embracing a large number of subsidiary companies each with substantial autonomy, and having in consequence only a very small headquarters staff. In addition, despite NBC being by far the largest single bus or coach operator, it co-exists with many local authority bus operators and several thousand small private firms. Moreover, the Traffic Commissioners have substantial powers to prevent or delay modifications to services. Thus the NBC (and the Scottish Transport Group) has never, since its comparatively recent foundation, had the *formal* power of BR to determine almost all of the details of its passenger services. There can be no doubt, however, that the NBC pattern of operation, with local services separately planned, financed and regulated in each region of the country, is the pattern of the future and it is notable that BR local passenger services have, especially since 1974, emulated bus services in being modified in response to local authority and even to informal community initiatives.

5 THE TRAFFIC COMMISSIONERS

The influence exercised upon rural accessibility by the various bodies considered above, derives in large part from their role as agents of service provision. The Traffic Commissioners, in contrast, exercise a purely regulatory role but their importance is nonetheless substantial. Their powers in the field of rural public transport derive from the 1930 and 1960 Road Traffic Acts discussed earlier in this chapter. They are organized on a regional basis: in each of eleven traffic areas there is a full-time Traffic Commissioner assisted by unpaid Assistant Traffic Commissioners and a clerical staff.

They have many functions, but in the field of passenger transport they are responsible for licensing public service vehicles and their drivers. This role, with an eye principally to safety considerations, is uncontentious. But they also influence the quality and quantity of public road transport by their power to issue or withhold 'road service licences' relating to specific routes or services. In carrying out this function the Traffic Commissioners require precise details of the routes, times and fares of the proposed services and hear any objections from other operators and from the relevant local authorities. Applications are judged with reference to 'the public interest' and to 'the needs of the area': the central question considered is whether the apparent need for the proposed route is already adequately served. If it *is* deemed to be adequately served, the proposal will normally be rejected.

Controversy concerning this function of the Traffic Commissioners stems from the fact that the road service licensing system was designed to protect the reliable operator (and thereby the public) from 'fly by night' operators, in a highly competitive and basically profitable situation. Also, the system was designed at a time when there was scope for imposing a social conscience on operators by requiring them to cross-subsidize any unprofitable rural services from the proceeds of their urban services. Neither of these premises is valid in the 1970s. Rural transport planning has become more a matter of seeking ways of plugging the increasingly serious gaps in provision — rather than of adjudicating between keen rivals.

It would be wrong to imply that the Traffic Commissioners are unsympathetic to the problems of the rural areas. But it is nonetheless likely that their powers and their style of working — with quasi-judicial hearings attended by applicants and objectors often assisted by legal counsel — inhibits innovation and local initiative. It is also true that, rather like the British land-use planner, their powers are permissive and negative, rather than promotional and positive. They can disallow modifications to existing services or the introduction of new services, but they cannot prevent operators from wholly abandoning services and they cannot, of course, require that new services be launched. It follows that they cannot, therefore, give to the public the guarantee of continuity which is their basic purpose.

The body which comes nearest to being able to provide such a guarantee is, following the 1968 Transport Act and the 1972 Local Government Act, the county council. It is the county council which has the power to subsidize and the responsibility to coordinate, and it is the county council which has, or should have, the resources and the will to evaluate alternative transport proposals against objectives relating to cost and to social need. Thus, there is clearly a degree of overlap between the roles of the Traffic Commissioners and the county councils which would surely not exist if the system were being planned *de novo*. There is a strong case either for abolishing road service licensing altogether in basically unprofitable areas, or for vesting these powers in the county council. Opponents of this view would argue that much greater instability would result given the political vagaries of local government and also that intercounty transport coordination would become more difficult. But these disadvantages might well be prices worth paying — if more effective 'accessibility planning' became possible as a result.

6 CONSUMER BODIES

The consumer of public transport in rural areas can, in theory, make his voice heard via the political process of local government elections and lobbying, via informal pressure groups and in consumer organizations. Official consumer bodies exist with regard to the main nationalized industries. Those which bear most closely on rural accessibility are the Transport Users' Consultative Committees (TUCCs) and the Post Office Users' National Council (POUNC). Each considers a wide range of issues relevant to rural accessibility, notably the TUCC's investigations into the 'hardship' caused by rail closures and its efforts to get detailed re-timings of trains, and POUNC's concern with rural sub-post office closures, the removal of public telephone kiosks, and the implications of postal delivery and collection patterns for possible post-bus operations.

It can be argued that the TUCCs, like the Traffic Commissioners, are not entirely suited to current needs. Aspects of their operation which have caused adverse comment include the immense secrecy surrounding the substance of their investigations in connection with rail closures, the use of 'hardship' as sufficient condition for refusing a rail closure and (perhaps even more controversially) the failure to consider benefits *other* than hardship-avoidance in recommending the retention of a rail link — for example, substantial inconvenience or the route's possible economic benefits to the locality as a whole through its handling of tourist or commuter traffic.

7 THE PRIVATE SECTOR

Private sector firms (both within and outside the transport sector) have enormous influence upon the accessibility that rural residents enjoy. Their distinctive characteristic, of course, is that they tend to be less motivated *directly* by goals of public service and more by commercial viability. But this is a crude generalization and there are many exceptions.

The *independent bus operators* play a very important role in many rural areas. There is little evidence of scale economies in the bus operating industry and small private operators often enjoy lower average costs than the large NBC subsidiaries: they tend to buy secondhand vehicles which are often adequate for rural areas, to have lower overheads, to employ family labour which is generally more amenable to the split shifts that peak-hour working implies, and to be able to redeploy on to garage or maintenance work any staff not actually operating the vehicles at a given time. Most independent operators undertake a variety of work. School contract work tends to be their 'bread and butter', with private hire work providing the 'jam'. Stage services are generally · considered to be the least lucrative. The economic advantages enjoyed by many such firms, coupled with their greater potential for intimate local knowledge, gives them a viable complementary role alongside the larger NBC subsidiaries.

Other private firms play important roles in the provision of rural services, particularly in the retail sector. The role of the village shopkeeper has already been discussed (chapter 2). Again there is an important distinction between 'the little man' who often operates as much for social as for commercial reasons and big firms such as the nationwide retailing chains or the major breweries. Decision-making by the latter, as it affects rural areas, is an under-researched area, particularly as the closure of village pubs and shops can have serious consequences and because the scale economies and organizational efficiency of certain large firms might allow them to operate in rural areas if they so chose.

In addition, of course, all firms which operate in rural areas, irrespective of the nature of their business, are important as employers. Decisions concerning workplace location, working hours (including shift and flexible working arrangements) and the provision of transport for the journey to work all have direct implications for accessibility.

Inter-agency interaction

Dominant themes of the preceding discussion have been the multiplicity of the agencies which affect rural accessibility, and the complexity and unplanned nature of their interaction. Often individual agencies take decisions with the best of intentions but in ignorance of the ripples of effects which spread out to encompass the domains of other agencies and eventually the accessibility that a variety of rural residents enjoy. A simple matrix (figure 5.2) in which the two axes are each a simplified list of the relevant agencies, illustrates the complexity of the inter-action. A cross in the matrix denotes interaction in a way deemed to be both direct and significant in its effect upon accessibility.

By way of illustration it may be useful to take one agency in some detail, the *independent bus operators* (row and column 9). Some of the bodies which they affect or are affected by are indicated in the matrix, namely:

(i) *the county education department:* the independent operators can strongly influence the department's policy options and, in turn, their ability to offer off-peak services is often dependent upon their having 'bread and butter' schools contract work;

	County education dept	County planning dept	County social services dept	County surveyor's dept	District council	Parish council	British Rail	National Bus Co.	Independent bus firms	Regional health authority	Post Office Corporation	Traffic Commissioners	Dept of Environment	Dept of Transport	Private retailers
County education dept															
County planning dept	X														
County social services dept		X													
County surveyor's dept	X	X													
District council	X	X	X	X											
Parish council	X	X		X											
British Rail		X		X	X										
National Bus Co.	X	X		X	X	X	X								
Independent bus firms	X	X		X	X		X	X							
Regional health authy		X	X	X	X				X						
Post Office Corpn		X	X	X		X									
Traffic Commissioners	X		X	X	X	X	X	X	X	X					
Dept of Environment		X			X	X									
Dept of Transport				X	X		X	X	X			X	X		
Private retailers		X		X	X		X	X			X			X	

Figure 5.2 The interaction of some agencies relevant to personal accessibility in rural areas
(x: impact in a direct and significant way relevant to personal accessibility.)

(ii) *the county planning department,* which affects the bus operators by influencing the spatial distribution of population, schools, workplaces, etc.;

(iii) *the county surveyor's department,* which has responsibility for the county transport policy and the payment of subsidies;

(iv) *the district councils,* which have some powers in the field of public transport, but which indirectly affect the independent bus operators by their policies on council house location and by local planning decisions;

(v) *British Rail and the NBC subsidiaries,* which comprise the other major elements in public transport operation and afford both competition and some cooperation — the impact is thus two-way;

(vi) *the Traffic Commissioners*, whose decisions are constrained by, and directly influence, the services provided by the independent bus operators;

(vii) *the Department of Transport*, which directly affects the independent operators by the execution of its financial and regulatory powers;

(viii) *private retailers*, whose operations are affected by the routeing and timings of scheduled services and shopping excursions, and who can themselves commission excursion services.

Taking the matrix as a whole, two principal features emerge. First, although none of the agencies interacts with fewer than five other agencies, each of the following interact with ten or more and thus appear to be particularly well 'linked in' to the informal organizational system which affects rural accessibility: the county planning and surveyor's departments, the district councils, the National Bus Company and the Traffic Commissioners. It certainly appears that any 'corporate initiative' in this field should usefully build upon the key position of the county planning and surveyor's departments. Second, of the many interactions, relatively few occur in a manner which is explored and formalized in the TPP and structure planning processes.

Agencies and accessibility: some concluding remarks

Before proceeding to examine the financial resources at the disposal of these various agencies for the alleviation of inaccessibility, a number of points relating to their roles, powers and interaction may usefully be drawn together.

(i) Accessibility in rural areas is affected by a large number of autonomous or effectively autonomous agencies. Some affect the resident's *ability* to travel, others his *need* to travel by influencing the pattern of population and activity distribution.

(ii) Relevant decisions are often taken without proper regard for their accessibility implications. The latter are frequently not a central concern of the agency in question.

(iii) 'Ripples' of effects pass readily through the system, with other agencies becoming unwittingly involved.

(iv) No single agency is responsible for, or empowered to coordinate, all of the accessibility-relevant decisions that are taken. But the county councils come nearest to this central position. A full coordinating role is probably best vested in the county councils because of their existing planning and transport expenditure in relevant areas. A more corporate approach within the county councils would be a first step forward.

(v) But this corporate approach must be linked to a wider community planning initiative, in which other agencies and the public are systematically involved.

(vi) Central government should foster this wider view of coordination by means of the advice and directives that DoE and the Department of Transport give to the local authorities. There is also a need for awareness to be increased in other central government departments about the implications of many of their decisions for rural accessibility.

Financial resources

As outlined in chapter 2, the late 1970s provide a context in which central government seems intent to shift the emphasis of its spending from the 'shire' to the metropolitan counties. This points to a need to seek the attainment of objectives of improved accessibility in rural areas principally by the redeployment of resources rather than by their increase. This, in turn, suggests a need to know just how great are the resources presently being expended in providing some measure of accessibility for rural residents, and how far these resources are susceptible to redeployment. Unfortunately, the complexity of the accessibility issue and the mass of relevant agencies makes these questions both important and very difficult to answer. Below an attempt is made to begin this debate, for it is alas very much in its infancy, by taking in turn a national, county and local perspective.

1 A NATIONAL PERSPECTIVE

At the broadest level it is clear that we should consider expenditure in both the public and private sectors designed either to provide or to remove the need for personal mobility. *Some* areas of expenditure include:

	Public	*Private*
Mobility	Road construction and maintenance. Public transport subsidies. Schools and welfare transport. Tax relief on company cars.	The purchase and running of private cars. Public transport fare payments. Transport provided by employers etc.
Alternatives to mobility	Grants and subsidies for location in 'uneconomic' areas. Subsidies for rural postal services. Maintenance of small village schools etc.	Payments for postal and telephone services. Payment of higher prices in village shops. Diseconomies arising from operating rural branch factories for reasons of labour supply.

Another way of trying to appreciate the scale and complexity of relevant expenditure is to concentrate on the financial *flows* which link five elements of the relevant systems, these elements being central and local government, public corporations, private firms and households. Again it is possible to be only indicative rather than comprehensive, but figure 5.3 sets out a few flows which affect the quality of access in rural areas. The point is simply that the magnitude of many of these flows (e.g., VAT payments by village shopkeepers and the 'vehicle excise duty' paid by private motorists) has *not* been explicitly determined with the needs of the 'rural accessibility system' in mind. And variations in their magnitude, decided at a national level, can have substantial and unforeseen effects in rural areas.

It has not been possible to estimate total public expenditure, nationally, on the provision of transport in specifically rural areas (i.e., expenditure belonging in the 'top left' box in the above table). But taking a much narrower perspective, it is often pointed out that expenditure designed to support rural stage bus services (just one component of this total) is extremely small in comparison with state support of air and rail transport or of public transport in urban areas (White, 1976). In the financial year 1976-7 the government spent about £34 million on fuel tax

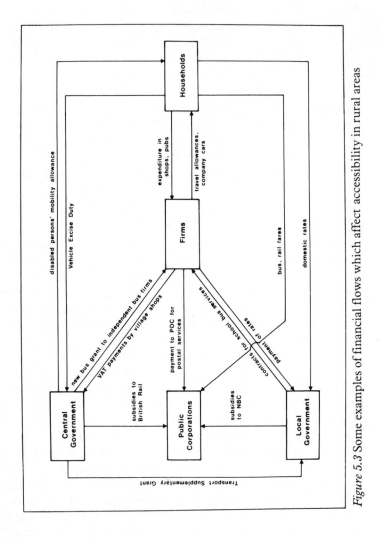

Figure 5.3 Some examples of financial flows which affect accessibility in rural areas

rebates to bus operators and about £32 million on 'new bus grants', both of these figures relating to national, not just rural, expenditure. In addition it approved expenditure by non-metropolitan county councils on public transport subsidies (almost entirely bus subsidies) totalling £33 million — and much of this must have been directed to essentially urban services such as those of Nottingham. In other words, the cost to the taxpayer and ratepayer of maintaining all of Britain's unprofitable rural bus services is not vast — it is to be measured in tens of millions of pounds compared, for example, with the level of government support for British Rail's passenger services which currently runs at around £300 million.

Alternatively we can refer to two interesting estimates by White (1974). He calculated that at that time the three sources of rural bus subsidy cited in the previous paragraph totalled under £20 million. And he estimated that the cost of maintaining all 100 million rural bus-miles lost between 1961 and 1973 would also have been only of the order of £20 million. Of course these figures are now dated and are in any case only part of a total picture which includes school bus services, etc., but they are useful in demonstrating that the drain on the nation's resources accounted for by the rural bus is by no means enormous, given the severity of the social problems involved.

2 A COUNTY PERSPECTIVE

In the UEA study an attempt was made to set this direct support of the rural accessibility in the broader context of indirect, even concealed, support. This attempt focused on net public expenditure, both capital and current, in the field of transport within a single county, namely Norfolk. The figures all relate to the financial year 1974-5.

The county surveyor's department was easily the largest single spender:

Road maintenance and improvements	£4,908,000
Winter maintenance	£360,000
Subsidies to NBC subsidiary and independent bus companies	£69,000
(note: the last figure rose by 1976 to over £250,000)	
Construction and major improvement of roads	£2,929,000
(excluding DoE trunk road schemes, which are considered below)	

The county education department spent £950,000 on schools transport, subdivided as:

Primary education	£111,000
Secondary education	£602,000
Special education	£122,000
Further education	£115,000

Much of this was paid to independent bus operators providing daily school services on contract. In addition, a proportion was spent subsidizing, or reimbursing, travel on scheduled British Rail, NBC or independent bus services.

The social services department spent £178,000 on their transport account. Most of this was incurred in transporting people to and from day centres and similar establishments. The department has a small fleet of minibuses of its own, but there is considerable reliance upon volunteers for this work, whose expenses are reimbursed.

More minor sums included £16,000 on the capital and operating costs of *mobile libraries*. Six or seven drivers were employed, and the addition of their salaries presumably took the total to at least £30,000.

To these sums could be added the salaries of county council officers involved in transport planning (e.g., in the organization of schools transport or of bus subsidies) and the amount spent on reimbursing county council staff for travel within the county on official business. Much of the latter may be construed as travel incurred in taking services to the county's residents. *The social services department*, for example, spent £136,000 of which 77 per cent went directly to staff involved in fieldwork and community care.

The district councils' direct contribution to mobility in the same period consisted of some £21,000 paid towards bus subsidies. In addition, some district councils operated concessionary bus fares schemes.

The Regional Health Authority financed personal mobility in a variety of ways but quantitatively the most important item was expenditure on ambulance services — estimated at £1,100,000. (About 90 per cent of journeys by ambulance are non-emergency and so perhaps £1 million may be considered to be relevant to the 'total rural transport account'). Other particularly significant items were the voluntary car service which relies on volunteer drivers whose expenses are met on a mileage basis, and doctors' travelling expenses. The 'Rural Practices Fund', which exists to defray the travelling expenses incurred by doctors in rural practices, currently runs at about £4 million (Countryside Review Committee, 1977): it is not known how much of this goes to Norfolk.

Similarly, the *Department of Health and Social Security* reimbursed the travelling expenses of a number of 'needy' people who had made trips necessary on medical or social reasons — but this sum is not thought to have been very substantial.

The other government body directly concerned with mobility was the *Department of the Environment* (relevant expenditure has since been transferred to the Department of Transport). First, there was the construction of new and improved sections of defined *trunk roads*: Norfolk's total for 1974-5 was estimated to be about £3 million. Second, *trunk road maintenance* (carried out by the county council on an agency basis) amounted to £3,045,000 in that year. Third were subsidies to unremunerative *British Rail* passenger operations, paid under the Transport Act 1968. British Rail would not disclose the precise proportion relating to *Norfolk* (and this proportion will be even more hidden now that public subsidy payments to British Rail are no longer linked to specific lines) but an estimate for 1974 was reached in the following way:

Norwich — coast group of lines (entirely within Norfolk)	£742,000	= £742,000
East Anglia/Midlands/North group (about 10% within Norfolk)	£941,000 x 10%	= £94,000
Cambridge group (about 40% within Norfolk)	£1,069,000 x 40%	= £428,000

This gives a rough total of around £1.25 million in 1974, or perhaps £1.5 million in 1975.

A summary of the estimated costs set out in the preceding paragraphs follows: it must be stressed again that the data relate to 1974-5:

(current)	Norfolk county council	£7½ million	
	Norfolk district councils	(insignifi-cant)	
	Regional Health Authority	£1½ million	£14 million
	D.H.S.S.	(unknown)	
	Dept of Environment	£4½ million	
(capital)	Norfolk county council	£3 million	£6 million
	Dept of Environment	£3 million	

This crude analysis of net expenditure in Norfolk by public authorities on personal mobility arrives therefore at an estimate of some £20 million in 1974-5 — somewhat over £30 p.a. per resident. Rapid inflation and real cost increases will already have greatly raised these figures. The true figure cannot be *less* than £20 million: it could be very much higher if other public agencies are included. For example the UEA research team ignored the Post Office Corporation whose transport-related expenditure in Norfolk must be considerable, and some at least of whose vehicles could in principle be made available to the travelling public.

3 A LOCAL PERSPECTIVE

Further exploratory work on the range of resources relevant to the rural accessibility problem was carried out by the UEA research team in relation to one small area of Norfolk, namely the rural area surrounding the small town of North Walsham. (This area extends over about 100 square miles and has a population of about 9,000. The reader is again referred to Moseley *et al.* (1977) for a full consideration of sources and methodology.) The estimates again relate to 1974-5.

In the field of public transport/mobile services·the following items of expenditure were estimated:

Stage-bus services (subsidized under Section 34 of	
1968 Act)	£13,000
Schools transport	£29,000
Mobile library	£8,000
Post Office collection and delivery vehicles	£22,000
Non-emergency hospital transport	£8,000
Social services transport	£3,000

These figures are, again, partial in that they ignore the subsidized rail service which crosses the area, as well as expenditure on road maintenance, etc. They also exclude, of course, both private transport expenditure and expenditure on 'fixed location services' which may reasonably be seen as substituting for public transport expenditure to some extent.

Regarding the latter, and by way of example, the research team estimated the annual current costs of certain services located in or primarily serving the study area. (In the figures given below allowance has been made for any lack of correspondence between the study area and the various catchment zones.)

Primary schools	£244,000
Secondary schools	£218,000
Libraries	£17,000
General medical practice	£41,000
Dental service	£24,000
Ante-natal care	£5,000

What is simply not known, and it is this which should properly be set alongside the transport figures given previously, is the proportion of this expenditure which arises from the deliberate provision of rural services in units which are smaller than the optimum economic size, so as to offset some of the accessibility problems implicit in a rural settlement structure. For example, how much is the primary education bill the product of maintaining very small village schools? Logically this sum belongs alongside the schools' transport bill in any estimate of total rural accessibility related expenditure. (Chapter 7 takes this a little further.)

Conclusion

The first and most obvious conclusion to be drawn from the preceding exercise in informed guesswork is that further research needs to be done! This is not simply the tired conclusion that follows most inadequate academic exercises but a real call for further detailed work examining costs not in relation to specific services but in relation to a fundamental goal, namely that of accessibility. Such an analysis would provide a proper basis for the urgent decisions which must be taken if progress is to be made at a time of only minimal growth in resources.

But what is already clear is that in the wider context of publicly financed rural transport expenditure, subsidies paid to continue unremunerative bus services are a drop in the ocean. Indeed, why such payments should be considered to be 'subsidies' while others, listed above, are accepted as 'payments for a public service' is far from clear. This is not to criticize county councils for looking searchingly at their Section 34 subsidy payments. But it is to suggest that in looking for cost-effectiveness in achieving basic standards of accessibility for their constituents their field of vision should be very much wider: corporate planning, with the shifting of resources so as to meet previously defined accessibility objectives, becomes all the more vital in a time of financial stringency.

The problem, of course, is that so much of the relevant expenditure is spread amongst a range of ill-coordinated bodies. As a core objective for public policy, 'accessibility' is not alone in straddling conventional service providing agencies and units of accountancy ('amenity', 'environment' and other quality-of-life objectives are similarly placed). But the need for improved coordination between the relevant agencies is no less urgent for that. Chapter 8 returns to this theme.

6
Personal transport—
options and experiments

How are the problems of accessibility, experienced by many rural residents, to be solved? Basically there are four sorts of policy which need consideration: to facilitate the mobility of the person, to make the service itself mobile, to induce the person to live nearer to the service, or to provide the service in a more accessible place. These options are set out diagrammatically in figure 6.1. In this chapter we are concerned only with the first of these alternatives, that is to say with the various ways in which the mobility of disadvantaged rural residents might be improved. The following chapter looks at the other three alternatives.

As will become clear there is a vast 'shopping list' of potential transport policies, from subsidizing conventional bus services to organizing car-sharing clubs. Some are already in widespread operation; some are at present experimental and in selected areas only; others are merely ideas. Some are novel and evolving, for example, bus services incorporating demand-actuated route diversions, others subsume a great degree of local variation — 'car sharing', for example, can mean very different things in terms of the availability, convenience and organization of the scheme. It is certainly too easy to jump to conclusions about the suitability of possible policies on the basis of very few observations — the dangers of excessive enthusiasm or prejudice are all too obvious in the transport world.

It is difficult, therefore, to evaluate the various options in the absence of a specific geographical context and precise operational details. Context is all important: the success or failure of an experimental scheme will depend on the nature of the people in

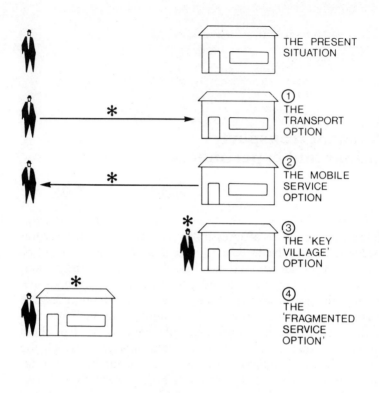

THE PRESENT
SITUATION

① THE TRANSPORT OPTION

② THE MOBILE SERVICE OPTION

③ THE 'KEY VILLAGE' OPTION

④ THE 'FRAGMENTED SERVICE OPTION'

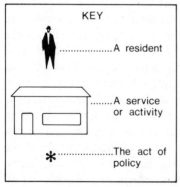

KEY

................A resident

........A service or activity

*...................The act of policy

Figure 6.1 The rural accessibility policy options

the area — their numbers, composition and attitudes — the environment provided by the settlement structure and existing transport provision, the administrative and financial context provided by the various agencies involved, and a host of other factors.

And in evaluating any proposed scheme there is a mass of questions which need to be posed. What are its aims? Who will benefit and who will lose? Who pays and by what means? Is it viable in the existing legal and administrative context? If not can these be effectively changed? Is it likely to be politically and socially acceptable in the given area? What community resources of voluntary labour and organizational expertise are needed, if any? How much time must elapse before success or failure can be reasonably assessed? What complementary policies will be needed? What other policies or objectives might be adversely affected by the scheme? These are, in effect, technical questions designed to establish whether the proposed scheme can effectively provide a reasonable increase in accessibility at an acceptable economic and social cost. But there is a political question too: for example, the technical question 'can a post bus provide a modest level of service at low cost?' must be followed by 'is a modest level really what we want?'

Two further points should be made by way of introduction. First, it is tempting to categorize schemes as 'conventional' or 'unconventional'. Those which use small vehicles and/or volunteer labour and/or a flexible route and timetable tend to be considered 'unconventional', and those which have none or perhaps only one of these attributes, 'conventional'. Probably, however, it is best to avoid such name-tags as they often generate unwarranted enthusiasm or antagonism in some quarters and because what may be 'unconventional' today may be 'conventional' tomorrow and vice versa. The second point concerns the need for experiments. There is a limit to the amount of desk-based evaluation that can usefully be carried out: eventually the proposed scheme must be implemented and evaluated on the ground. There is a need, then, for properly monitored experiments and for improved channels for communicating the results of these experiments. A number of such experiments are described at the end of the chapter.

The free market option

Rural public transport certainly does not operate in a free market context, and we must consider whether it should. As we have seen in the previous chapter, it is constrained (some would say 'retained') by the state in two particular ways. First the operation of bus services is *regulated*, in that would-be competitors must first obtain a road service licence from the Traffic Commissioners, a licence which is rarely granted if an existing service is deemed to be adequate. Second it is *subsidized* by three means: the fuel tax rebate, the new bus grant and an operational subsidy paid jointly by central and local government to selected loss-making services. The question that follows from this is basically a simple one: given that rural public transport is poor and is largely in the hands of semi-monopolistic public bodies, would it not be better to scrap the controls and subsidies and see what private enterprise can do?

On the face of it this seems an attractive proposition. One can envisage enterprising people organizing new minibus services, car-pools for payment, taxi services with payment shared between the users. Many long-established bus and rail services would go to the wall but services truly responsive to people's needs, and for which the public is prepared to pay, would replace them. People would be forced to make themselves more independent of public transport, by acquiring their own transport, by generating some community-based solution, or by moving out of the area. A more economically efficient settlement system and transport system would eventually emerge. And, in the process, large sums of money previously tied up in subsidies, would be released for other purposes. So runs the argument

The reality, however, would probably be rather different. The sums released by ending subsidies to rural bus operators would be quite small — see the estimates for the mid-1970s contained in chapter 5. Although this figure of around £20 million has increased significantly since then (see chapter 2) there is the point that the losses incurred by such services are often exaggerated by insufficiently sensitive accounting procedures. Certainly to use a single figure of the costs per mile of bus operation for both urban and rural routes places the rural areas in an unreasonably unfavourable light since the greater speeds possible on rural roads mean that labour productivity is higher (more bus-miles per man-hour) and in general there is in any case less wear and tear on the vehicles.

Another point is that although the total subsidy bill is not large, to remove it forthwith would inevitably impose quite substantial hardship on many rural people. Rees and Wragg (1975), for example, demonstrated that without any subsidy payments there would be virtually no inter-urban bus or rail services in mid-Wales. And for many people the options of buying a car or of moving home are effectively not open, for compelling economic reasons. People *are* gradually changing their habits so as to become less dependent on rural bus services, and perhaps one case for continuing subsidies is to make this transition less painful.

Some commentators would go further and suggest that the benefits which accrue to the community from retaining bus services through subsidy payments are substantially greater than the cost of the subsidies themselves. Car users, for example, may very rarely use their village bus but the value to them of having available a rudimentary bus service which they could if necessary fall back upon, is likely to be much greater than the fare they would pay if they did in fact make emergency use of it. Trench (1975) has cogently argued that the gap between a service's receipts and its costs of operation (i.e., the financial loss incurred) is only one basis for deciding whether and how much to subsidize. Much more valid, and much more difficult to calculate, is the size of the benefit to society, and it is possible to envisage a situation in which a service should be subsidized *beyond* the break-even point if in doing so proportionally greater benefits to society were obtained. That, perhaps, may in practice seem a little fanciful but inevitably one is forced to ask, what is a 'subsidy' and what is a 'community decision to purchase a service'? In county halls up and down the country vehement opponents of subsidizing rural bus services would never consider that rural telephone, postal, police, education or sewerage services should pay their way.

All this is not to say that the precise form of regulation and subsidy that we have today is ideal — rather that unfettered free-market competition would be unlikely to provide a solution that would gain general acceptance as being socially or indeed economically desirable.

Stage bus services

Stage or 'stage carriage' bus services are those which operate to a specified timetable and upon which separate fares are payable — i.e., they comprise the great majority of bus services. We have already seen that as passengers are lost to the motorcar, such bus services have tended to decline. Operators have been forced to respond to a declining revenue by reducing the frequency or geographical extent of their service, by raising fares or by seeking subsidies — usually by doing all of these things. The problem is that cutting services and raising fares both loses further custom and causes social hardship, and that requests for subsidy may increasingly fall on deaf ears if there seems no end to the spiral of decline. It is possible to be rather fatalistic about the whole business and to say that technological advance is inevitable and the rural bus is now an anachronism. More reasonably it seems clear that the bus must give way to the car just as newspaper publishing, the cinema and radio have all had to cede ground to television. This, then, is to argue that in rural areas the bus must do what it is good at, and must aim to adapt to changing circumstances.

What it is good at, basically, is carrying fairly large numbers of people at predictable times along a common route. In short, it is well suited to peak movements of workers and schoolchildren if the origins and destinations of those people are not too geographically scattered. The problem is that such peak movements dictate both the size of the work force (and labour costs account for about three-quarters of all costs) and the size of the vehicle fleet. An important challenge, therefore, is to make proper use of both drivers and buses in off-peak periods. The attraction of these periods is that the marginal costs of operation are effectively very low because the driver and the other fixed costs of operation are already covered. In consequence one area of policy concerns the building up of off-peak excursion services. An excellent example is provided by the 'Cromer market bus' in Norfolk which provides off-peak shopping trips for many rural housewives at the expense of Cromer traders. The bus is always fully loaded and the marginal costs per passenger are very low. Building up 'bus clubs', in which members pay an annual subscription that entitles them to use an off-peak scheduled service without further charge, is another possibility presently in operation in the Louth-Horncastle area of Lincolnshire.

Five other ways of resisting the apparently inevitable decline of the rural stage services should be mentioned: market research, marketing and information, better coordination, technical/operational developments and fares policy.

1 MARKET RESEARCH

It is often said that the small independent bus operator, living amongst the people whom he sets out to serve, is best placed for gauging latent demand. But the large operators, subsidiaries of the National Bus Company, have achieved some success by using formal market research techniques. These involve not just on-vehicle surveys of users, but doorstep interviews of non-users. The Eastern Counties Omnibus Company, for instance, has instigated a rolling programme of revising its routes and schedules, area by area, on the basis of market research — and it reports some increase in bus loadings as a result. Market research is probably as valuable in a contracting market situation as it is when growth is anticipated.

2 MARKETING AND INFORMATION

Knowing your market is not the same as getting it to know you. Many, but by no means all, operators are increasingly concerned to do something about their poor image and the general climate of ignorance in which the public exists. One long-needed innovation here is to get away from conventional booklet timetables which are a source of great fascination to the enthusiast but often mean little to the sort of people who comprise the bulk of the bus operator's market. Advances must build on the would-be user's perception of space: he or she wants to know how a trip can be made from his or her particular village to alternative destinations at different times. Whether the service is operated by company x or company y is irrelevant — so too are considerations of where the vehicle has come from. Perhaps the need is not for conventional bus timetables, but for village-based readable statements of alternative ways of getting to different places.

3 BETTER COORDINATION

Already we have argued (chapter 5) that there is more to coordination than removing duplicatory services and knitting timetables
together. But advances even in this narrowly interpreted field of
coordination can bring substantial benefits. Where a small town
to large town rail service remains, for example, there seems little
point in duplicating it by bus services which would be more useful
feeding into it.

4 TECHNICAL/OPERATIONAL DEVELOPMENTS

Obviously, a major way of reducing operating costs in a labour
intensive industry is to reduce the labour force by introducing
one-man operations, but there is now little or no scope for further
savings in this direction. Vehicle design, particularly the
application of ergonomics to such things as step heights, seat
design and luggage space, is also likely to increase the attractive-
ness of bus services to those groups, such as the elderly and
housewives, most likely to need them.

5 FARES POLICY

Finally, there is the difficult business of pricing the services.
Fares have risen very substantially in recent years, even faster
than the retail price index and certainly faster than disposable
incomes. (See figure 2.5 for increase in consumer expenditure.)
Fare increases certainly lead to a loss of passengers, but the evidence does not support the popular view that this loss is so
substantial as to make fare increases self-defeating. White (1975),
reviewing the evidence on price-elasticity, concluded that a 10 per
cent fare increase in rural bus services tends to produce a 7 per
cent or 8 per cent fall in passenger miles and a 2-3 per cent increase
in revenue. What has to be decided, of course, is whether this
modest return is really worth the social costs involved — almost
certainly that figure of a 7 or 8 per cent decline conceals a good
deal of personal hardship.

On the other hand, it is hard to support calls radically to reduce
or even abolish fares. There can, of course, be no such thing as

free public transport — the issue is how it should be paid for — and a move towards substantially lower rural bus fares is in effect a move towards favouring those people already having the good fortune to live on a bus route. Almost certainly, in the event of extra money being made available for rural transport, this should go to help people who presently have no, or only a very rudimentary, service. But this is not to say that valuable social and even revenue-generating results could not be gained by more careful price discrimination according to trip purpose, trip time and the identity of the person. Low fares for off-peak shopping trips by the elderly provide an example.

Rural rail services

There is considerable scope for debate amongst accountants concerning how much of British Rail's costs should be charged against particular services, but even on the most favourable assumptions rural rail services will generally cost more than comparable bus services. This is still true despite the elimination of the most uneconomic rural railways in an extended period, from the 1920s to the 1960s, when first bus and then car competition began to bite. Any proposals to increase rural rail services, for example by reopening lines or stations, opening new halts, or providing extra trains on existing lines, would be unlikely to interest either British Rail or central government and would therefore be a local authority responsibility. Indeed the indications (Department of Transport, 1977) are that the powers and responsibilities of county councils with regard to railways within their boundaries, will increase in future years. This being so, there could be welcome moves towards a greater integration of road and rail travel at the local level, with less inter-urban duplication and better bus-rail interchanges. This is certainly the avowed policy of Norfolk County Council — a county which still retains a number of Norwich-focused local rail services.

Demand-actuated transport

A 'demand actuated' transport service is one whose route and/or timing responds at least in part to *ad hoc* passenger requests. The *taxi*, of course, is the commonest form of such transport, it being characteristically geared to the needs of a single client or small group of clients. Taxis are quite extensively used in rural Britain, often by pre-arranged groups of children or adults making school or shopping trips. The problem is that per capita charges are high, indeed generally prohibitively so for most of the 'problem groups' described in an earlier chapter. One constraint is that taxi-sharing by strangers is effectively ruled out in Britain, as one passenger must bear the full responsibility for the fare. Thus the knitting together of a number of separate 'desire-lines' into a single taxi trip is not at present a legal possibility in rural Britain.

'*Dial-a-ride*', in which a would-be passenger telephones for a flexibly routed minibus to divert to or near his or her house, is superficially an attractive proposition for rural areas, where competition from schedules services is minimal, and the social need for mobility high. But dial-a-ride is expensive to operate, with passengers per hour being inevitably few and with the high costs of the central control unit which links passenger and driver and constantly readjusts routes and times. Oxley (1976) reviewed the twelve schemes that operated in Britain between 1972 and 1976 and found that five had been discontinued and that none could approach financial viability. Nearly all were set in urban or suburban locations, and the greater scatter of population in rural areas would only make things worse. What is more, in such areas the greatest need for such a service would probably come from people without telephones and with high resistance to the sort of fare-levels that even loss-making services have had to charge else-where.

But, if dial-a-ride seems a non-starter for rural Britain, this is not to rule out every possible kind of demand-actuated transport system. A low cost/low quality system could be imagined, running only in off-peak hours and thereby using already-paid-for vehicles and personnel, with routes being determined by a combination of telephone and postcard messages and 'standing orders' (see the St Ives midibus, pp.135-6). Alternatively the selective *diversion of scheduled bus services* offers real possibilities. The idea is to achieve an optimal combination of directness between towns A and B with the provision of a service to neigh-bouring villages and hamlets lying close to the route. At present many bus services *always* divert to *certain* of these neighbouring hamlets. This is a source of annoyance and of wasted resources if the diversion is abortive, and it fails to provide any sort of service to other hamlets with equal claims for inclusion. The key dilemma, 'to divert or not to divert', can be determined in one of two ways — in a 'drop-me-off' scheme or in a 'pick-me-up' scheme.

The former is much the simpler. The passenger merely asks the driver to divert to his or her home village. No complicated communications technology is required and the service can prove particularly valuable as it is often on the homeward trip that the passenger is tired, burdened with shopping, or travelling late in the day. A 'pick-me-up' arrangement is more difficult. It involves the same problems of communication that were observed for dial-a-ride. But for any pre-meditated trip this need not be too difficult — a postcard or phone call to the central office is all that is required. A general, but again not insurmountable, problem with all such schemes is that a precise timetable becomes impossible if too many diversions are permitted. Probably a system of 'latest and earliest arrival times' would have to be introduced, but this indeterminacy might well be a price worth paying.

Multipurpose transport

The possibility of using one vehicle and one driver to perform a number of apparently distinct tasks is particularly attractive in a rural context. This is because there is a wide range of separate agencies independently operating transport in such areas, whether to carry passengers, for example, hospital out-patients and the clients of social services departments, or goods, such as groceries, newspapers, or mail. Indivisibilities of supply often produce spare capacity in rural areas — it simply is not possible to provide half a postman and half a mail van in the remoter areas, even though that may be all the service warrants! The interesting possibility for personal mobility is this: if a vehicle and driver already has to service a remote rural area then why not attach to it a passenger service at a very small additional cost?

In Scandinavia there are many examples of transport services with a 50:50 division of passenger and goods space. In Austria and Germany postbuses are extremely common and are often virtually indistinguishable from conventional buses in their speed, directness of route and passenger capacity. 'Common carrier', or combined goods and passenger services, were once common in Britain and though this is unusual now many bus companies are happy to provide a parcel delivery service. A feature of the St Ives midibus scheme is the bus driver's being entrusted with shopping orders and medical prescriptions and with his dropping off the goods on his return journey. And in Scotland the Borders Regional Council has actively investigated the possibility of cooperating with the local health authority in a scheme which would have mail, stores, goods and paying passengers moved between their various establishments by a single fleet of vehicles.

However, space permits a discussion only of the *postbus* system, which has become widely established in Scotland but only to a limited extent south of the border. The Post Office has an obligation to deliver mail to everyone in the country, which, given a common tariff irrespective of location, must mean a tacit acceptance of subsidy in the remoter rural areas. The Scottish Postal Board has now recognized that in consequence they have a very useful resource — vehicle and driver — which could be put to greater use by incorporating a passenger transport service.

The first postbus was introduced in Scotland in 1971 and by 1976 there were 84 separate services, covering 2500 miles and carrying over 100,000 passengers per year very largely in areas previously without any public transport at all (figure 6.2). The one-hundredth scheme was introduced in 1977 and further expansion is under way. In England, events have moved much more slowly, but schemes near Dorking, Canterbury and Colchester suggest a potential even within the metropolitan southeast.

The guidelines used by the Post Office Corporation prior to the introduction of a new service are as follows: there should be a demand for the service; it should not make a loss (i.e., receipts should cover the marginal costs incurred by transforming the mail service into a mail/passenger service); it should not compete with an existing transport operator; and it should be compatible with the POC's prime task of collecting and delivering mail. In addition, of course, the service has to have the blessing of the corporation's employees, and happily in Scotland the Post Office Unions see the schemes as a valuable community service which, moreover, bolster their case for continuing to deliver mail in the remotest areas.

Scottish postbuses make a small profit for the Scottish Postal Board: most run without financial support from the local authority except where the latter has requested extra services. New vehicles are generally required, but the minibuses purchased are eligible for the 'new bus grant' and the fuel tax rebate is payable for passenger services. Other costs relate to the training of drivers to Public Service Vehicle licence standard, and the organization and administration of the services. In short, the marginal costs of conversion are not great and loadings in consequence do not have to be high for a service to break even.

Typically, postbuses link a rural area with an urban centre. Four trips are normal: a slow trip out from the town in early morning, a fast trip back in mid-morning, a fast trip out in early afternoon and a late afternoon slow return trip with mail being collected. Clearly it is the second and third of these trips which are most attractive to the rural resident, providing the possibility of a reasonably speedy return shopping trip to town.

What is to prevent the postbus from becoming a major mode of transport in rural Britain? First, the timings described above: these are clearly not suitable for school or work trips which tend to focus on the town when the mailvan is going in the opposite direction, and vice versa. Second, the circuitous and time-consuming routes make them unattractive except to the most captive passenger. These constraints, however, could in principle be relaxed if the public and the unions were to accept the collection and delivery of mail at different times of the day and, perhaps, at reduced frequency. The mail collection and delivery service is understandably held to be paramount by the POC, with the passenger being the poor relation. A case could certainly be made for a reassessment of these relative priorities, though the POC could hardly be expected to initiate such a reassessment itself.

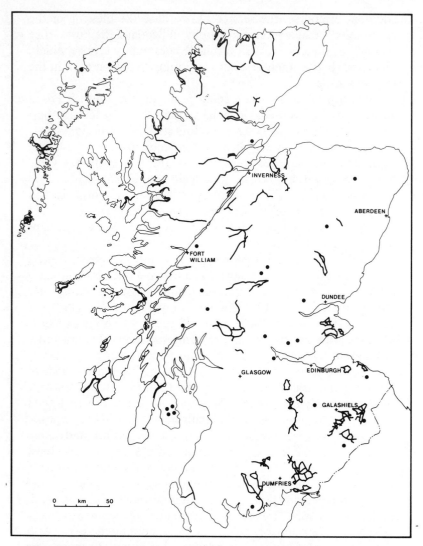

Figure 6.2 Scottish postbus services (The routes of the first 84 services (to summer 1976) are indicated by continuous lines. The approximate locations of more recent schemes (to spring 1978) are indicated by black circles)
Source: Carpenter (1976) and more recent information kindly provided by the Scottish Postal Board

Schoolbuses

Another transport service which has inevitably to be provided on a large scale in rural areas and which could possibly form the basis of a more widely available passenger transport is the 'schoolbus'. Local education authorities have a legal obligation to ensure the availability of transport for schoolchildren who have to travel more than three miles to school (two miles in the case of children under eight years). Many travel by scheduled stage bus or train services, others by taxi or by some sort of private car scheme, but in rural areas of most importance are the bus services run exclusively for schoolchildren, either by the county council or by an independent operator under contract to the county council.

Schoolbuses are of central importance to the whole rural accessibility question. To begin with, they account for a much greater proportion of county council expenditure than does the subsidy of stage bus services. A typical non-metropolitan county council spends well in excess of one million pounds annually on its schools transport service. And, because of its scale and peak-hour nature, the demand for schools transport in large part determines the size of the rural bus fleet. And as noted in the previous chapter, independent bus operators see their school contracts as the 'bread and butter' of their business, providing a stable base upon which to add the 'jam' of excursion traffic. Further, a decision to run a schoolbus in circumstances when it would be possible to channel school trips on to a suitable stage bus service clearly undermines the viability of the latter and may generate demands for its subsidy by the county council under a different spending head.

Many county councils now recognize the need for a much closer coordination of schools transport and conventional stage services: some, such as Devon, have given the same transport coordinating officer responsibility for both. On the face of it, it makes good sense to allow adults to use schoolbuses at least when there is no reasonable alternative transport available. But, although this is explicitly permitted under section 30 of the 1968 Transport Act, in practice schoolbuses are nearly always exclusively reserved for schoolchildren. Most services are painstakingly routed to run at or very near to full capacity; there is the problem that they run for only about 40 weeks per year;

and if fare-paying passengers *are* carried then the legal concession that three children may be squeezed into two seats apparently becomes invalid. Nevertheless, if rural transport services were planned *in toto* rather than in quite watertight compartments then room would surely be found on 'school' buses for adults living in bus-less villages, if only by prior arrangement.

A rather more radical approach to the closer integration of schools transport with the mainstream of rural transport services has recently been adopted by Oxfordshire County Council (1976). Its 'extended school contract scheme' involves linking school contracts with a requirement that the operator also runs certain off-peak services which are specified by groups of local people in conjunction with the county council. If these off-peak services are not commercially viable, then a subsidy becomes payable, but it is the council's belief that greater value for money can be obtained from payments of this kind than from the subsidy of conventional stage services — a subsidy which it intends to discontinue.

Another way of reducing the total bill for schools' transport is to stagger school hours: as has already been stated the peak demand for schoolbus services in large part fixes the number of vehicles and drivers needed. Even a quite small variation in school hours, say within half an hour of the typical 0900 and 1600 start and finish times, could permit individual vehicles and drivers to account for a higher proportion of total traffic and thereby permit also a reduction in their numbers. It seems attractive but of course there are snags: staggering could not be so great as to impinge substantially on the contract services which are run for work trips and there can be quite serious social implications if anything more than a very modest change in school hours is implemented. Such implications include the effects upon other household members, particularly the mother, if in effect they are required to be at home at different times (see figure 4.6 on the 'time-space realm' of the rural housewife).

The private car

In looking to postbuses and schoolbuses to meet some of the transport needs of isolated rural residents we are in effect seeking ways of escaping the labour costs of conventional bus services. Another way of doing this is to rely on unpaid drivers. Two interesting possibilities present themselves here: first, making much greater use of the privately owned motor car; second, operating community-run transport services. The present sub-section concentrates on the former.

The authors of the Devon and West Suffolk studies referred to earlier (Department of Environment 1971 a and b) were very keen on the possibility of putting the car to greater use in rural areas. The latter concluded by asking 'is it too much to hope in this compassionate society of ours that a small amount of [the car's] almost unlimited potential can be diverted, now and then, to solve the hardship of the old, the young, and the needy?' Certainly the car is an extremely attractive resource: in rural areas it is both extremely plentiful and uniquely flexible in terms of both route and timing.

One suggestion has been to try to raise car ownership levels still higher in rural areas by means of some form of subsidy, for example a lower rate of vehicle excise duty for rural residents or some rebate of fuel tax. Such schemes, however, would be extremely difficult to administer and would still do nothing for the hardcore disadvantaged whose ages or incomes preclude car ownership even with such assistance. Inevitably then, in looking to the car in rural areas, we must seek ways of extending its advantages by some form of 'car sharing' arrangement.

There is, of course, a considerable history of volunteers making themselves and their cars available for socially useful work in rural areas — either for no payment at all, or, more recently, for their mileage-related expenditure. Such volunteers have frequently been organized by the WRVS, Red Cross, Women's Institute or some such organization. The 'Social Car Service' operated by the old Lindsey County Council is a case in point. Financed and controlled by the council, although operated by the voluntary organizations, the service was designed to help people 'in need' to make medical trips and to visit friends and relatives in hospital.

Any move to extend such an approach more widely in the community runs up against a number of problems of a sociological nature. First, information: an efficient 'clearing-house' would be needed to put into contact those offering and those needing a lift. Second, attitudes: most motorists would be happy to help a friend in occasional need, but most also value the privacy that private motoring affords and would not like to feel obliged to give lifts on a regular basis particularly if they felt they were 'taken for granted'. Similarly, would-be recipients of lifts might feel too proud to accept 'charity' and experience a feeling of indebtedness even if they made payment. Yet a really effective system of car-sharing would need to be able to guarantee regular opportunities for travel and to be put on a financial footing acceptable to both parties.

The simplest and probably commonest form of car sharing is the informal 'car pool' with two or more people taking it in turn to give each other free lifts to and from work. If no payment is involved then there is certainly nothing illegal about this and it does not violate normal car insurance policies. At present operating largely on an *ad hoc* basis, it is not difficult to predict much greater involvement by employers, consumer groups or parish councils acting as 'linkmen'.

There are, however, problems if a scheme extends to include payment by the passenger. Regular car-sharing in return for payment by passengers is banned by the 1960 Road Traffic Act, although to the extent that the practice is infrequent, small-scale and unadvertised, it may apparently be legal. (The 1978 Transport Bill promises further concessions, see pp. 190-1.) Insurance is the other potential problem, although the British Insurance Association declared in 1975 that contributions by passengers towards petrol expenses would not be held to infringe the 'hiring' exclusion of normal private car policies.

Clearly, looking to the long term, there is no reason why any legal problems could not be swept away, and in certain experimental areas motorists are presently being permitted to offer lifts to all and sundry in return for payment (see p.138). But the 'everything affects everything else' problem has to be remembered. If car sharing for payment were to catch on in a big way, then this could sound the final death knell of the rural bus — and is this really desirable? (One independent bus operator, for example, suggested that every work trip accommodated by a car sharing arrangement effectively cost him £100 per year: a sobering thought.) Again, then, a need is demonstrated for planning the rural transport system in a truly integrated way.

Minibuses

Most people, on seeing conventional rural bus services operate for much of the day with only a handful of paying passengers on board, must at some stage have thought that it would surely be better to run a minibus instead. Certainly the twelve-seater minibus seems an attractive proposition, being easier to drive, better suited to narrow rural roads, and able to travel at faster speeds overall. And its operating costs — particularly fuel and maintenance — must be lower than those of the conventional bus. The problem, however, is that labour costs form about 70 per cent of bus operating costs so that the overall saving is small. And this saving may be wiped out completely if the operator already has to have a conventional bus on the road to cater for peak hour (work or school) trips. Surprisingly, then, it may well make better economic sense to run a 41-seat vehicle on off-peak services attracting just enough passengers to cover their marginal costs, than to buy and run a minibus to carry the same passengers.

The legal position regarding minibus services has been simplified in recent years. Under section 30 of the 1968 Transport Act, the Traffic Commissioners can grant permits (in lieu of road service licences) for minibus services carrying up to 12 passengers along routes otherwise without public transport. But in practice commercially run scheduled minibus services are rare — doubtless for the economic reasons set out above. The few that there are tend to be in areas topographically unsuited to the larger vehicle, e.g., the Lake District's Mountain Goat Service, or else, of course, operated principally for another purpose, e.g. the postbus, discussed on pp. 125-7.

Minibuses operated by schools or by religious or voluntary bodies on a non-profitmaking basis no longer require road service and PSV licences following the 1977 Minibus Act. This new law, the result of a private member's bill, should help organizations with their own vehicles to provide a basic level of mobility for particular groups, but for those who hire or borrow vehicles the situation is apparently still legally complicated (Dods, 1978).

Some experimental schemes

It remains to consider a number of innovatory rural transport schemes introduced in the period 1976-8. As experiments, they might in due course founder or be radically modified. But they embody characteristics of organization and operation which may well become much more commonplace in the remoter areas of Britain in the 1980s.

1 THE NORTH NORFOLK 'COMMUNITY BUS'

This scheme serves six small villages near Holt in North Norfolk which have a total population of about 600, no shop, no other public transport and only one pub and two sub-post offices between them. Three parties are involved. The Eastern Counties Omnibus Company (a subsidiary of the National Bus Company) provides and maintains the twelve-seater minibus, has trained the drivers, looks after licensing and insurance matters and provides overall supervision. The Norfolk County Council financially underwrites the scheme, though, having accepted the likelihood of a small loss in the initial stages, it expects the service to break even in due course. The 'community', i.e. the residents of the six villages, provide two inputs: first, an organizing committee with, fortunately, an energetic retired schoolmaster as its secretary; second, a pool of about 20 volunteer drivers (some from outside the immediate area), all PSV licence holders trained by the 'bus company', and all prepared to drive two or three hours each week on a rota basis.

The organizing committee now operates both scheduled services (under a 'section 30' permit — see p. 129) and excursion traffic. The former include regular schools transport (paid for by parents because the distance is less than the two or three miles minimum for county council support), scheduled shopping trips into the small towns of Holt and Fakenham, and trips to a general practitioner's surgery financially underwritten by the doctor himself. Excursion traffic, which makes an important contribution to revenue, has its own organizer and includes evening and weekend trips to such destinations as the coast and the cinemas and theatres of Norwich.

Fares in 1976 were set at 10, 15 and 20 pence and receipts are paid in to one of the post offices for onward transmission to the county council. A monitoring exercise undertaken at the end of the first year revealed that about 140 passengers per week were carried and that revenue and costs were each running at about £30 per week. The service had worked very smoothly and had kept to the timetable. Both the morale of the drivers and passengers loadings had kept up well during the winter months and an intangible improvement in community spirit was reported.

In short, the Norfolk community bus is a most promising experiment, but three problems impede the widespread adoption of such a scheme in poorly served areas. First, the road service licensing legislation requires that such a service fits very carefully into the existing network: in short it must not compete with an existing service. Second, although the Transport and General Workers Union gave the North Norfolk scheme their blessing, the use of volunteer drivers would almost certainly be opposed if any scheme were proposed for an area where a commercially operated service runs or could be expected to run. Third, it is by no means clear that all remote rural areas have the quantity and quality of personnel able not only to drive the vehicle but, perhaps more important, to organize and manage its operation. (Chapter 7 considers in greater detail the problems involved in relying on community resources for the provision of transport services.)

2 THE ST IVES MIDIBUS

Another experimental rural transport service operated by the Eastern Counties Omnibus Company cuts across the categorization of transport services used in this chapter. It is quite different from the North Norfolk scheme in that it uses neither volunteer labour nor local volunteer management. The 25-seater vehicle is operated by two paid drivers based at the small Cambridgeshire town of St Ives. The scheme began in May 1976 in an area on the northernmost edge of London's commuter hinterland containing small, dispersed settlements and only trunk bus and rail services of little use for local movement.

At the time of writing (late 1977) seven distinct services are operated by the bus, during each five-day week (see figure 6.3).

Two of these are run daily, the other five operate once or twice each week. First, there is a *'door-to-door commuter link'* between the St Ives area and Huntingdon railway station. This service runs twice each morning and evening and connects with fast trains to and from Kings Cross. Second, there is a daily *'work and school service'* between Alconbury and Huntingdon. In addition, off-peak services are as follows:

Monday: a *'shop or ride service'* into St Ives. Residents of a number of villages near St Ives can make the trip themselves or entrust their orders to the driver who, for a small charge, will do the shopping for them in the two-hour stop-over in the town.

Tuesday and Friday: a *'dial-a-bus service'* focused on Sawtry — a small town with inter-urban transport connections. Passengers must telephone a central office before a certain time in the morning, and the driver himself telephones in for instructions. Expensive communications equipment is thereby avoided.

Tuesday and Friday: on the same day a *'local service'* within Sawtry is run during the stop-over time of the dial-a-bus.

Wednesday: a *'surgery service'*, focused on Yaxley health centre. Patients may book a seat at the same time as arranging an appointment with their doctor.

Thursday: a *'market day service'* into Oundle, run on conventional lines.

This experimental scheme has been financially underwritten by Cambridgeshire and Northamptonshire county councils. It costs about £250 per week to run, nearly half of this being accounted for by the drivers' wages. In the first year a small loss was sustained.

3 THE 'RURAL TRANSPORT
EXPERIMENTAL SCHEMES' (RUTEX)

All of the various experimental schemes described above — postbuses, community transport, dial-a-bus, etc. — must obviously operate within the framework of legislation designed to protect existing transport operators. In order to see in a practical way what might be achieved if this constraint were removed, the government recently introduced legislation (the Passenger Vehicles (Experimental Areas) Act 1977) which provides for the

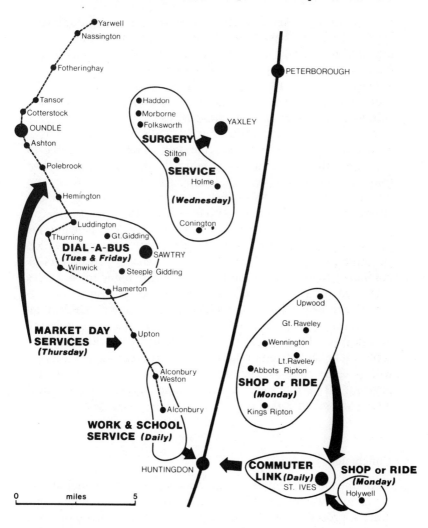

Figure 6.3 The St Ives midibus service
Source: Eastern Counties Omnibus Co. Ltd

temporary relaxation of some of the present licensing code within designated experimental areas. Thus enabled, the Department of Transport, together with the Scottish and Welsh Offices, has established experimental rural transport schemes in parts of

Devon, North Yorkshire, Southern Ayrshire and Dyfed. Sixteen approved schemes have been put into practice (not all of them in fact needing the new enabling legislation) and it is worth listing them in full in order to show their variety.

They include: two flexible route services using small professionally driven buses and offering pick-up on demand; a volunteer-driven community minibus, also with flexible routeing; three variants on a new form of operation involving shared hire-cars charging each passenger separately at rates comparable to bus fares (these will provide highly flexible, low capital cost feeder services to local centres, to longer distance bus services and (in Devon) to local rail services); four schemes involving the use of private cars authorized to charge fares, so as to provide an organized transport service in areas of very low demand for public transport; two hospital transport schemes, which (according to local need) may involve hire-cars, private cars or minibuses, to tackle the problems of people living in remote areas who need to get to urban hospitals whether as visitors or out-patients; three postbus services (one linked to one of the flexible-route minibus schemes); and an emergency car service, catering for unexpected and urgent transport needs. In addition, a special zone will be designated in the Devon study area, where motorists will be able to make private arrangements to give lifts for payment. It is too soon to say whether any, or all, of these interesting schemes will warrant more widespread operation.

Conclusion

The 'transport option' — giving carless people more mobility — is only one way of attacking the rural accessibility problem, and other approaches are reviewed in the next chapter. Even so, there is a wide variety of possible schemes contained under that broad umbrella. A need will almost certainly remain for a basic network of scheduled stage bus services, but such services are economically unsuited to operation over most of rural Britain away from the large villages and small towns and their inter-connecting routes. Something else must be developed in such areas, and almost certainly this 'something' will vary from place to place: there is no panacea on the horizon. Whichever schemes are developed, however, certain key needs stand out — particularly imaginative management and some form of popular involvement in the schemes' operation.

7
Alternatives and complements

Making it easier for carless rural residents to travel to the services they need is the obvious way of trying to solve the rural accessibility problem. But, as the previous chapter has shown, such an approach involves a whole range of social and economic problems. Perhaps, therefore, it might be useful to complement that approach with alternative policies which in certain circumstances might even very largely remove the need for movement by the disadvantaged groups that we have defined. Most possibilities were set out graphically in Figure 6.1 and in this chapter we consider three main areas of policy — taking the activity to the people (mobile services and telecommunications), locating the activity nearer to the people, and locating the people nearer to the activity. In addition, attention is focused upon a number of policies which act upon the time dimension (by modifying personal time-budgets and the 'opening hours' of different activities) and upon the scope for involving the community in the various areas of policy discussed in this and the preceding chapter.

Mobile services and telecommunications

Two particular mobile services — shops and libraries — are well known in many rural areas, though the former at least has been in decline in recent years. The question that has to be asked is whether such services could and should be made more attractive to the consumer, perhaps with state assistance, and whether their

scope might be extended into other more unusual fields —
mobile post offices, medical surgeries, dentists and advice
bureaux perhaps.

Mobile shops tend increasingly to be unattractive in the context
of modern shopping demands. The range of goods on sale has to
be limited given space limitations, and given the time involved in
travelling from place to place only a relatively small proportion of
the day can be spent actually trading. This and the increase in
fuel costs in recent years have contributed to prices being
significantly higher than those in urban supermarkets. And so,
despite the decline of its obvious competitor, the village shop, the
mobile shop has itself declined in recent years, with the rise in car
ownership, the associated trend towards infrequent multipurpose
shopping trips to town, and the rise in female activity rates which
has reduced the number of women 'stuck in the villages'.
Nevertheless, there are clear attractions of such a service for the
captive rural resident, particularly the elderly, and a case could
be made for some limited state assistance, for example with the
capital costs of new vehicles to be used predominantly in rural
areas.

It is impossible here to discuss the whole range of possibly
mobile services. But the mobile playgroup, or *'playbus'*, is an
interesting possibility. Facilities for pre-school children are poor
in rural areas and it is not just young children who benefit from
regular contact in this way: isolated rural mothers frequently
express a need for such a facility. Some voluntary groups have
already experimented in this field and one can envisage a
converted double-decker bus serving, say, five villages a week,
with the downstairs area being used as a coffee bar and as a
vehicle (literally!) for publicising community events, while
upstairs could be reserved as a children's play area. What would
be the costs, and the benefits of such a scheme? There is no
readily available answer to this question, and this is a deficiency
which ought to be rectified.

The *'meals-on-wheels'* service, staffed largely by volunteers but
with local authority assistance, is a more established example of a
service being taken to the homes of people in need — in this case
hot meals to the housebound elderly. In rural Norfolk, however,
only about 3000 people were getting the service in 1974 and most
got only one or two meals a week. The well-served villages tended

to be those with a relatively large population, with population growth and an above-average proportion of two-car households. Volunteers are in short supply in the remoter rural areas and the greater distance between clients in such areas raises the question of the most appropriate way of meeting the need: big, school-based, kitchens cooking in bulk but involving a good deal of travel by the deliverers; or more numerous, smaller and more labour-intensive kitchens; or a system of home-helps actually cooking the meals in the clients' homes. The meals-on-wheels service encapsulates in microcosm all the issues of economics, society and space which make up the rural accessibility problems (Stockford, 1978).

A fourth kind of service which might be put on wheels and taken to people's homes or at least to their immediate vicinity, is *information provision*. A service provided in the Cleator Moor area of Cumbria illustrates what is possible (Butcher *et al.* 1976). This is a semi-rural, semi-industrial, largely working-class area with low levels of car ownership and telephone penetration and with only very rudimentary bus services and fixed-location services. Into this context the Cumbria Community Development Project introduced their 'information and action van' — a Commer 1500 van with a high roof conversion and containing a desk, seats, filing cabinet, and a series of local volunteers each acting as driver and helper. Its function was two-fold — to disseminate information and to take up people's problems — a sort of mobile citizens' advice bureau and social services office rolled into one. Success was only partial. The vehicle was conspicuous and offered only a limited amount of privacy: it became stigmatized as 'the problem van'. But its proponents eventually concluded that a useful service *could* be provided if it used one full-time, non-local, worker whose integrity was respected and if a radio-phone link were provided so that problems could be immediately referred to the appropriate agency.

However, if the task is to disseminate information then why not use *telecommunications* and take the service right into people's homes? Research at Lanchester Polytechnic (Clark and Unwin, 1977) suggests that while our need for information increases as society becomes more complex, the traditional purveyors of information in rural areas, people who could be turned to for advice on a wide range of matters such as the village policeman, clergyman or postmaster/mistress, are decreasing in numbers and becoming less able to offer the sophisticated information required. Such 'community leaders' have given way to professionals who tend, because of the large populations needed to support them, to be located in towns, and often in different towns. So information from the Citizens' Advice Bureau, the Department of Employment and the Department of Health and Social Security, for example, may often be gained only by time-consuming and expensive visits to different centres.

One suggestion for alleviating this problem is to increase telephone penetration in rural areas by subsidising the cost of installing or using the telephone — perhaps for elderly people only. Another interesting possibility is to build on the fact that 92 per cent of British households have a television set (compared with only 50-60 per cent with a telephone). The Post Office, in conjunction with the BBC and IBA has been developing systems called 'Viewdata' or 'Teletext' whereby the consumer sitting in his own home can call up pages of information to be received and displayed on a modified 625 line television set. Access to the system is by means of a small key pad — not unlike an electronic calculator in appearance — or via a telephone. A recent *Observer* review (23 October 1977) reported that in early 1978 about 1000 people would be taking part in a market trial to test public reaction, each person having access to 100,000 'pages' of information. There seems to be no technical reason why the rural resident should not be able to call up information about local jobs, social security entitlements, local planning applications, bus and train times, etc. But inevitably there will be problems. First, cost: initially the modified sets will cost about twice as much as a colour TV, but obviously this could come down substantially with mass production. Second, consumer resistance: will old ladies in rural Britain prove to be as adept in finding out the price of butter in North Walsham or the times of the buses to Norwich as will businessmen wanting the latest City prices or the time of the next flight to Miami? Third, will the receipt of information by rural residents *replace* the need for mobility, or will it simply render that mobility more fruitful? In the final analysis it is all very well knowing that there is a suitable job available for you in Norwich or that butter is a penny cheaper in Tesco's but you still need to get there to make use of the information. Telecommunications can contribute to the alleviation of rural isolation, but are unlikely, alone, to remove it.

The location of 'activities'

1 OPTIONS AND POWERS

If we consider how the modification of the pattern of service provision in rural areas might improve the access to those services that people enjoy, then two possibilities present themselves. The first option is to try to *resist* the forces which are gradually leading to the withdrawal of services from the small villages in favour of the urban centres. The second option, perhaps surprisingly, is to 'bend with the wind' — i.e., to *accept* the potency of such forces but at the same time to shape the way they find expression on the ground so that access to those services is improved. Any consideration of these two options, however, must be preceded by some appreciation of the limited powers of the planners to achieve whatever pattern is desired (a subject already raised in chapter 5).

There are really two points to be made here. The first is that the planners' powers are largely indicative, permissive and negative. 'Indicative' in the sense that decisions on the disposition of infrastructure — roads, sewers, water supply, schools, etc. — provide a framework in which the private sector can make its own decisions on the location of factories, shops and other service outlets. There is a mass of literature which establishes that private sector location decisions tend to be made on inadequate evidence of costs and benefits, and as much for psycho-sociological reasons as for hardheaded reasons of profit maximization — in short that 'economic man' exists only in the textbooks — but, in the long run and to a certain extent, the pattern of such decisions is surely influenced by the guiding hand of the public sector. The planner's powers are 'permissive and negative' in that he cannot require a chemist to open a shop or a manufacturer to establish his factory in a given location. He can only *permit* him to do so and simultaneously try to wield the stick that the refusal of planning permission elsewhere implies.

The second point about the planner's powers, again raised in an earlier chapter, relates to the difficulty of orchestrating a consistent set of policies even within the public sector. 'The planner', in the sense of the planning officer and his committee in county hall, may designate certain villages as suitable or unsuitable for expansion or for service provision. But those employed by the district council, the regional water authority, the area health authority and the Post Office Corporation — responsible respectively for the location of council housing, sewerage and water supply, hospital provision and the operation of post offices, and equally worthy of the designation 'planners' — may have their own ideas. Such are the problems of implementing a desirable spatial pattern of service provision, even if a 'desirable pattern' can be determined.

It is, then, difficult for society, through its various agencies, to resist the forces that tend to push service provision to higher levels of the settlement hierarchy — schooling for young children from small to large villages, hospital provision from small to large towns, etc. Not only is the domain of the planner largely limited to public sector services (schools and post offices, not pubs and shops) but there are real costs involved in fragmenting provision between a number of small settlements as the next sub-section makes clear. Nevertheless, there are also significant costs involved in *accepting* the concentration tendency. These latter costs take two forms: first, there are those associated with the transition period during which the concentration of facilities takes place quite rapidly with compensatory housing concentration failing to keep pace; second, are those associated with minorities who suffer isolation despite the *aggregate* improvement in accessibility to facilities that the policy of concentrating facilities and people eventually brings about.

2 OPTION ONE: BOLSTERING UP THE SMALLER VILLAGES

Such is the case for trying to maintain service provision in the remoter areas: concentration or 'key village' policies can be socially regressive if carless rural residents are not actively provided for. How might such bolstering be achieved, with regard to the principal *private* sector service, namely the shop? A number of possibilities present themselves. First, the fact that village shop and sub-post office facilities are frequently provided in the same premises (as noted in chapter 2) could be built upon as it gives the public sector some 'leverage'. The Post Office Corporation could be required to give existing village retailers 'first refusal' in seeking any new outlet for post office provision. Alternatively the state could undertake to pay a higher salary to a sub-postmaster/mistress in return for an assurance that a basic retailing service would also be provided. (In this context, it is interesting that a rural subsidy scheme is now in operation to try to stem the decline of chemists' shops in rural areas. Supplementary payments are made to pharmacists providing essential services in such areas so as to secure their continued operation as NHS contractors; Countryside Review Committee, 1977). Another possibility is to afford some form of tax relief to village shopkeepers — local rates and VAT are very frequent sources of complaint by such people, as are any capital gains tax or capital transfer tax which may be levied if their business is sold or passed on to a relative. A further area of possible influence relates to urban retailing. A proposed urban, or more particularly 'out-of-town', retail development could be resisted by the planning authorities if it implied a real threat to village retailing. Or such developments could be approved with a requirement that the retailer cross-subsidises some village retailing outlets. Finally, the state could directly involve itself in village retailing either by the direct payment of a subsidy, geared to precise obligations imposed upon the proprietor regarding price and range of stock, or by outright municipalization.

Inevitably, with all of these options, the problem is 'where to draw the line'. If certain village shopkeepers are to be favourably treated in some way, why not others? And why not the urban corner shop as well? In any case not all of these options are presently viable under existing legislation. But these problems do not mean that the option should not be considered once it has been accepted that there is little fundamental difference between on the one hand subsidizing a bus service so that the rural resident might make a shopping trip and on the other hand removing the need to make that trip by some form of public support of the local shop.

In similar vein, it is open as a policy possibility to promote more vigorously the provision of new employment in rural areas. Many local authorities are already directly involved in this field by providing serviced industrial sites and advance factories and by means of a variety of industrial promotion exercises. Their efforts could be stepped up but to the extent that they are directly in competition with one another the exercise does become a rather fruitless 'zero-sum game'. And if rural industrial development is to be attempted by attracting mobile firms rather than by fostering indigenous enterprise then the local authority may in fact be putting its urban and rural areas into competition with one another. Certainly there are potent economic forces drawing most industrial development to small towns at least, if not to the major urban centres. Even the Development Commission, the principal agency charged with developing the English rural economy (the Scottish and Welsh Development Agencies have parallel roles), feels a need to concentrate its largesse geographically. Within its 'Special Investment Areas' which are earmarked for favourable treatment in the provision of advance factories and other inducements, attention is generally confined to a few well-chosen small towns and large villages (Development Commission, 1977). It seems that the vision beloved of many environmental and rural pressure groups of every small village having a modest endowment of workshop or cottage-type industry will prove to be elusive unless technological developments cause a fundamental reassessment of the scale economies which exist in most manufacturing processes.

3 OPTION TWO: KEY VILLAGES

The alternative location policy, then, is to 'swim with the tide' of concentration but to fashion the trend in a socially less regressive way than would occur if market forces and pure financial accounting were allowed to rule unhindered. If it is accepted that the number of outlets in rural areas must continue to decline (whether they be shops, pubs, school or whatever) there are basically two ways of proceeding. Either some degree of scatter could be retained (with village A keeping its pub, village B its post office, village C its primary school, etc.) or else all activities could be pulled into a *single* settlement (either A, B, or C) as far as this proved possible. In accessibility terms, it is hard to see any case for the former option, denying as it does any real possibility of developing a viable public transport system and thereby the chance for carless people to have some of the mobility and scope for making multi-purpose trips that car-owners presently enjoy. This is one strong case for a 'key village' policy, involving the deliberate spatial concentration of service provision.

Another strand of the 'concentration argument' relates, of course, to the greater ability to provide services that comes from clustering the population and services close together. This leads to the notion of 'thresholds'. It is difficult, if not impossible given the dynamic nature of the situation, to prescribe precise minimum population thresholds needed to support certain services, but there have, of course, been numerous attempts to estimate these empirically. For example, a Cambridgeshire County Council study (1968) reported that 2000-3000 inhabitants were needed before a hardware store or electrical goods shop became viable, while Green (1971) suggested that in Norfolk at least 4000 people are needed to support a chemist's shop and 6000 a three-doctor medical practice.

Such thresholds tend to rise through time and not surprisingly, then, there is by now a considerable history of 'key village' type policies in most if not all of Britain's rural counties (Woodruffe, 1976). The Norfolk structure plan, for example (Norfolk County Council, 1977), designates 6 of the county's small towns as industrial 'growth centres' with scope for substantial residential development, 12 small towns and large villages as 'local centres' suitable for more modest employment and population growth and about 25 large villages as 'service centres'. In the author's view the dual arguments of economic efficiency and of the potential for improved public transport that such a strategy implies, are sufficiently persuasive to warrant its support so long as adequate complementary policies are in fact pursued in the areas discriminated against. Such complementary policies are the subject of much of this and the preceding chapter.

The location of people

One such complementary policy, of course, relates to the gradual clustering of much of the rural population around the main points of service provision. This is not only justified in terms of personal accessibility, but also by the resultant lower per capita costs of basic service and utility provision. This latter argument seems incontrovertible, at least given present technology. Shaw's recent research (1976) is relevant: he examined the costs of public service provision given alternative dispositions of population growth in north east Norfolk. He estimated the capital and current costs of providing various public utility services given either the concentration of new growth in the largest settlements only, or its dispersal amongst all the villages in his study area. The latter strategy proved to be 50 per cent more expensive for telecommunications, 30 per cent more for water supply and 20 per cent more for electricity. (The costs for sewerage disposal were complicated by considerations of alternative technologies: septic tanks, small-scale village 'package' treatment schemes and conventional sewerage schemes gave different results.)

In similar vein, the Countryside Review Committee (1977) highlights some other hidden costs of population scatter. Given the Post Office's obligation to operate daily delivery services even in the remotest areas, it is not surprising that their average costs in rural areas are much higher, the Review Committee stating that a real delivery cost of 18 pence per letter is not unusual in such areas. Further, while the national average number of patients on a doctor's list is 2350, in rural areas it is only 2000, and we have already noted (chapter 5) the costs of the 'Rural Practices Fund' which exists to defray the higher travelling expenses of rural doctors. Telephone call boxes are often uneconomic in rural areas: the Review Committee states that in 1970 many had receipts of less than £10 compared with an average annual running cost per box of about £300. The higher per capita costs of small village schools has already been referred to (chapters 2 and 5).

All this is not to say that cost should be the sole criterion in the gradual restructuring of the rural settlement pattern. But when the conclusions from such economic analyses point in the same direction as do analyses of the very restricted levels of accessibility of carless rural residents, then the case for actively promoting the spatial concentration of population, if only at a local, intervillage, scale, becomes a very strong one.

But can it be done? More specifically, how far is it possible to 'steer' such people towards the better served locations by means of policies relating to housing construction and tenure?

As far as the construction of new rural housing is concerned there are two particularly important points. First, about 80 per cent of it is undertaken by the private sector (Rogers, 1976) and second, there is a good deal of pressure for development in the smaller, more poorly served villages, where land prices tend to be lower and where the environment may, at least superficially, appear particularly attractive for the urban retired and the commuter. A legacy of existing planning permissions makes it difficult to restrain development in these small villages to any great degree. Norfolk, for example, has 48 villages with existing permissions for 50 or more new residences, many of these villages not having been selected as service centres (Norfolk County Council, 1977). Indeed the same county witnessed particularly rapid population growth in its smallest settlements in the early 1970s, in contrast with an earlier trend. In the longer term, when many existing permissions will have lapsed in a climate unfavourable for new housebuilding, then the spatial pattern of housebuilding might be better wedded to that of service provision, but in the meantime a lot of people will inevitably have come to live in the remoter areas — not all of them with adequate use of a car.

But while society has some control at least over the location of new private-sector housing development, it has no influence over who purchases and subsequently occupies it. (Nor, of course, has it any influence over the identity of people who buy already existing properties in rural areas.) With only about 20 per cent of new building in rural areas being undertaken by the public sector and with a rented housing stock that is declining in absolute terms, this is a serious constraint inhibiting the development of socially progressive accessibility policies. Indeed, in the many rural areas where district councils have an ideological aversion to large-scale council house building programmes then this constraint will continue and perhaps intensify (Larkin, 1978).

As Rogers (1976) observed, the principal rural housing problem is no longer that of quality but of availability: it is chiefly 'demand' or ability to pay rather than some measure of 'need' which determines the occupation of the rural housing stock. Little is known about who actually moves into the key villages designated in rural planning policies, but it is possible to hypothesize that a high proportion are relatively long-distance and prosperous migrants from the urban areas rather than short-distance, disadvantaged migrants from neighbouring more poorly serviced rural areas.

Presumably some steps could be taken to alleviate this situation if district councils chose to step up their housebuilding programmes in the key villages. And in the allocation of such dwellings greater weight could be given to the *location* of the potential tenant's present accommodation as well as to such traditional factors as family size and the *quality* of that accommodation. More 'sheltered housing' in the key villages could be built and allocated primarily to elderly people from the outlying hamlets and remoter areas. In addition, much better information could be provided for potential migrants into the remoter areas from urban areas. It is not uncommon for a retired couple to move from suburban London to a remote East Anglian village and to express surprise on discovering that there is no bus service. It might be sensible to require house-vendors (or perhaps the local authority) to inform would-be immigrants of the basic realities of their chosen village prior to the house being purchased. The point is that it is often the public sector in the form of local authority social services departments which ultimately meet many of the costs of an ill-advised decision.

But, even if such policies were vigorously pursued there would inevitably remain many carless people living away from the key villages and interconnecting routes. So long as society continues to assume the provision of education, postal, medical, and emergency services irrespective of a person's location — and it is hard to argue that it should not — then some people will continue to live in the remoter areas despite great adversity. This points again to the need for complementary accessibility policies for these areas. The simple point of the present sub-section is that key village policies should certainly incorporate a real attempt to allow carless people to move into the key centre and to advise potentially carless people from other regions of the possible implications of their proposed move.

Time-dimension policies

The need for explicit and coordinated consideration of the time-dimension of the people-link-activity accessibility system tends to be appreciated much less than is the need to plan this system in its spatial dimension. A very useful conceptual framework within which to explore the possibilities of improving personal accessibility by manipulating the time-dimension, is provided by the Swedish school of time-geography. This was briefly reviewed in chapter 4. The diagram provided there (figure 4.6) makes the basic point that people are effectively 'trapped' within a 'time-space realm': we cannot seek the activities to which we require access either in 'forbidden' geographical territory (outside that area within which we can effectively travel) or in already-accounted-for time (for example during sleeping time, or time devoted to feeding the baby). The challenge of accessibility planning is to *expand* that time-space realm (by enlarging the area over which we can travel, or by reducing unwanted time commitments) or to pack more activities within it (e.g., by opening a village shop so that such an activity is no longer 'out-of-bounds' or by keeping the shop open in the evenings).

In the present section we consider only those policy elements which impinge directly on the time-dimension. The options considered relate either to people's *time budgets*, or to the '*opening hours*' of activities. The essential problem is that people's uncommitted time, or 'time-windows' (the time left over to perform activities outside the home or workplace) is frequently incongruent with the 'opening hours' which determine when those activities are available. This is particularly true in rural areas because of the considerable increase that trip-making can make to the amount of time already committed to other tasks and because of the infrequency of public transport links.

It is convenient then to consider two categories of time-related policy alternatives — relating respectively to personal time-budgets and to activity opening hours.

1 TIME-BUDGET POLICIES

The challenge here is to increase or rearrange the blocks of time that rural people have available for performing activities outside the home, or at least to increase their control over their total time-budgets. Thus one possibility, which might effectively raise people's ability to have access to activities which interest them, would be to reduce onerous incursions into the time they have available. Reducing the need for young mothers to spend two hours a day accompanying children to and from school is one example. So too is a system whereby workers can opt for a 10-hour, 4-day working week with the result that one weekday is available for other things. By increasing telephone availability it might be possible to reduce the amount of time wasted by having to visit information sources in person. Organizing, perhaps on a weekly basis, a village child-minding service so that mothers might make a shopping trip or span that trip over a lunch-time, is another possibility.

2 'OPENING-HOUR' POLICIES

How can the times at which activities are 'offered' to the public, be usefully and realistically rearranged? The following are some possibilities:

(i) *Clustering in time* activities which service different groups of people, so as to improve the viability of a public transport system. For example evening classes, cinema programmes and bingo sessions could all be made available at precisely the same time on the same day. (This policy presupposes, of course, the *spatial* clustering of these activities, and adds force to the case for key village or small town policies in which activities are concentrated in selected centres.)

(ii) *Making certain services available outside normal working hours.* For example the Saturday morning or late-evening opening of banks or local government offices, even on a once-monthly basis, could greatly assist people who are occupied during conventional opening hours. Similarly, extending hospital visiting or permitting visits at any time of the day could reduce the problems of people who have to rely on infrequent bus services.

(iii) *Staggering the timing of activities* which make intensive use of peak-hour transport facilities. The varying of school hours has already been discussed, and systems which allow flexible working hours provide another example. The problem is that although such policies can reduce the need for investment in transport infrastructure and in the case of the employee, allow him a greater degree of control over his daily routine, they are likely to have adverse side effects. Staggering school hours will affect parents' time-budgets in a way that might prove onerous: a parent might have to return from work earlier in order to welcome the child home. And in rural areas flexible working hours may in fact undermine the potential for a viable peak-hour transport system, rather than reduce the unwelcome pressure on it that is typical of urban areas.

(iv) *Careful coordination of public transport timings and of relevant 'opening hours'.* Of course most public transport operators already do their best in this respect. So do some providers of activities in rural areas, for example those medical practitioners who take care to arrange their surgery hours and their appointments schedule so as to fit in with bus timetables. But the general point is that the timing of a bus or rail link can be as important as its existence in effectively providing people with accessibility.

(v) *Having part-time outlets* in several locations, rather than a full-time outlet in one. The extreme form of such a policy is, of course, the mobile service (discussed pp.140-2) which serves, say, each of 40 places for one hour per week. At a more inter-mediate position between this and the conventional fixed location services, is a service resembling the 'periodic market' found in many developing countries. It might be useful to describe in some detail how such a scheme could work in practice, since it illustrates very nicely the need to integrate the three elements of time, location and transport in accessibility planning.

Essentially the idea is that peripatetic services in a district could congregate on a single weekday in each of a sequence of large villages. Those services for which the necessary threshold populations are too great to permit the operation of a full-time permanent fixed outlet in rural areas, but which are not totally immobile, might be provided in the following way (see figure 7.1):

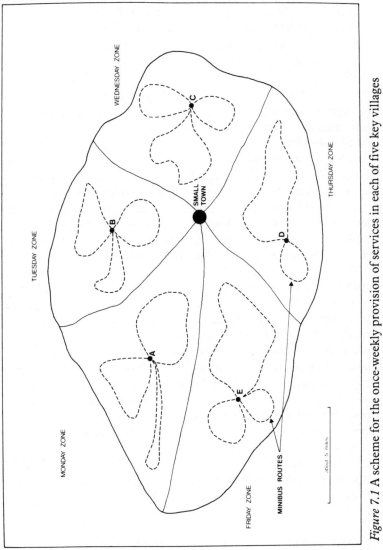

Figure 7.1 A scheme for the once-weekly provision of services in each of five key villages

(i) The area around a small town is divided into five zones, corresponding to successive weekdays;

(ii) a key village is selected within each zone to be the focus of a once-weekly local transport network and the location of a once-weekly public-sector 'market'. (In effect, this translates to the *village* scale and to the *public* sector, the rotation of *private* sector provision markets between *small towns*, typical of many rural areas.)

Thus, on Monday of each week, village A would be the location of, say: a post office, a citizens' advice bureau/local authority information outlet, a library, a doctor's surgery, a dentist, a family planning clinic, a bank. There could also be a mobile shop or even a mini-market of local produce, a tearoom or stall and other private sector activities. On Tuesday it would be village B's turn and so on. Some of the activities would be genuinely mobile (with the vehicles suitably equipped and drawn up in a central location in the village). Others would be located, for the day, in a building or buildings made available for the purpose — the back room of the village shop, or the village hall perhaps.

Such a scheme would bring to the residents of quite remote rural areas the chance of frequent easy access to quite high level services. And it would make very little demand on public transport. The key villages would themselves contain a large number of each zone's population and the rest of the zone's residents could be served on the appropriate day of the week by a single minibus which would be 'handed on' from zone to zone, day by day. On a 'one day a week' basis such a transport scheme might not exhaust the community's own volunteer driver resources but a professionally based 'minibus service', as in the St Ives scheme (chapter 6), might be preferable. One small modification would involve the scheme being held in abeyance on the market day of the central small town. Thus there would be just four sectors, and on the fifth day public transport would focus on the small town (as it frequently does in East Anglia).

3 TIME-DIMENSION POLICIES: A CONCLUSION

To conclude this consideration of 'time-policies' two final points may usefully be made:

(i) Many time-policies will have potentially adverse side effects — such as the possible constraints that staggered school hours might have on the time-budgets of the working mothers. Similarly the occasional Saturday morning opening of local government offices would impose an economic and social cost on those supplying the service. But so too might changes in policy of a more conventional type, such as the re-routing of buses or the implementation of a 'key village' policy.

(ii) There is no single agency charged with studying and co-ordinating the temporal availability of services — nothing, that is, comparable with the well-developed *spatial* planning function played by local authorities. But *when* an activity is available may be as crucial to the rural consumer as *where* it is available.

Community involvement

'Involving the public', as a policy option, cuts across the transport/location/time dimensions of policy which have provided the framework for this and the preceding chapter. It is possible to conceive of the public being directly involved in many of the policies described in this and the preceding chapter but such is the interest currently being shown in 'grass-roots' or 'community' solutions to the rural accessibility problem that these warrant integrated consideration. Recent years have witnessed not only an upsurge of public opinion in favour of greater involvement in decision-making at the local level, but also growing feeling that 'the community' comprises a resource of time, labour and expertise which could be more systematically tapped — that 'do-it-yourself' at the village scale may well make a real contribution to the alleviation of rural accessibility problems. Below we consider in what ways and to what extent such an approach constitutes a real alternative or at least a complement to the professional provision of services.

'Community involvement' can take a variety of forms. Taking examples from the transport field, we can envisage schemes run in partnership with official bodies (for example the Norfolk community bus scheme, described in chapter 6) and schemes which are wholly of a 'self-help' nature. The latter might be formal, for example a village 'transport club' of some sort, or informal as with neighbourly help with shopping or work trips. Further, the type of involvement can be supplementary, as with the provision of a local transport service feeding in to an inter-urban bus route, or else be largely self-contained as with a local transport scheme replacing an official service. More modestly, the community involvement might be nothing more than the transmission to appropriate bodies with executive power, of information gathered by means of a household survey in the village, or a process of liaison and pressure aimed at achieving the re-opening of a rural railway halt. And so in purpose, organization and function there is potentially a wide variety of forms of community involvement.

1 PRE-REQUISITES AND CONSTRAINTS

Community awareness of and involvement in schemes which alleviate access problems in rural areas is highly sporadic, geographically. What determines the genesis and subsequent success of such schemes? The chief factor is undoubtedly sociological: a necessary, but not sufficient, condition is the existence of a core person or small group of persons with the energy, time, administrative skills and personal qualities to conceive a viable scheme and, by motivating others, to ensure its successful operation. Such people are not uniformly distributed within rural areas and large, socially cohesive villages with a big middle-class element tend to have more than their 'fair share', though this important dimension of rural life certainly warrants further research. In addition to these key personnel, who in practice often tend to be doctors, schoolteachers, clergymen or retired professionals of either sex, there must usually be a pool of volunteers prepared to do 'the donkey work'. Further, all of these people must share a feeling that their work is not only socially useful but also a proper matter for their concern: a feeling that 'they' — the authorities — should properly provide the service can dissipate energies into useless protest.

In addition to these social and psychological factors there are, of course, those of a legal and economic nature. Certain legal constraints, though occasionally flouted, impede community action — for example the laws which forbid private motorists from driving 'for hire or reward', or which prevent 'bus clubs' from running services which compete with those of professional operators. Other schemes might flounder for economic reasons: if motorists are not reimbursed for out-of-pocket expenses incurred in transporting visitors to hospitals, then in time they might desist from so doing. Thus successful community action requires adequate personnel, and an appropriate legal and economic basis. A parsimonious state, intent on fostering such action rather than merely rendering it necessary, might usefully consider how it might foster or ameliorate each of these elements.

2 SOME EXAMPLES

It is useful to consider some specific areas in which community involvement is already a reality, or else has been suggested as worthy of experimental consideration.

Transport provision

Volunteers, sometimes working closely with professionals, may be involved in providing, or in helping to organize, transport for the carless. There are plenty of examples of 'social car schemes' in which volunteers are reimbursed the marginal costs of taking visitors to hospitals or the elderly to luncheon clubs, etc. More independent are village transport clubs which provide transport for their members either by organized car-pooling or by chartering buses to run on otherwise busless routes. Some rural employers provide minibuses which one of the employees uses to transport a number of people to work, and such an arrangement could be organized by a parish or district council given a potential clientele employed by different firms. The North Norfolk community bus service (chapter 6) provides a good example of volunteers and official bodies working closely together.

So much for volunteers helping to *provide* transport: they can also help to organize its provision by professionals. Oxfordshire County Council's rural transport policy, for example, is in large part founded upon the formation and operation of 'parish groups' of people who are expected to ascertain local needs and to advise the council on policy (Oxfordshire County Council, 1976). In particular their task is to determine what additions, if any, to the basic *unsubsidized* rural bus network, should be commissioned from independent bus operators as part of an 'extended school contract scheme' (a scheme, discussed in chapter 6, which links school contracts to a requirement to run certain off-peak services as well). These groups are encouraged to deal directly with the operators on as many operational matters as possible, and are kept informed of county policy and of any changes in the base network by means of frequent newsletters from the council's office in Oxford.

Information provision

Another way in which community involvement can be of value in rural areas concerns the collection and dissemination to residents of useful information. For example, the Department of Environment's West Suffolk study (1971b) suggested a scheme whereby suppliers and potential consumers of informal car lifts could be put in contact with each other by means of a register of planned trips kept in a public building such as a shop or post office.

Mobile services

Voluntary participation in policies which 'take the activity to the person' rather than vice versa, exists in a variety of forms. At one extreme is mere good neighbourliness with car owners doing shopping for their house-bound neighbours. At the other are schemes which involve official backing and financial support, such as the meals-on-wheels service. Possible policies include the promotion of 'errand running', perhaps with a roster of car drivers providing a shopping service similar to that provided by bus drivers in the St Ives midibus scheme (see chapter 6).

The location of residents

At first sight, no policies in the 'location of residents' category appear susceptible to community involvement. But perhaps rural residents and community organizations do have a potential role in fostering the sort of short-distance population movement discussed earlier in this chapter. This could take the form of improving the welcome accorded to people who move into key villages and small towns from remoter rural areas. Where such migration is encouraged as part of a wider policy for alleviating inaccessibility, the people who arrive are likely to be relatively immobile and in need of some help with the problems of settling in.

The location of activities

Policies relating to the 'location of activities' which might be amenable to community involvement include attempts collectively to finance or even operate such facilities as pubs or shops. So significant is the pub as a focus of village community life that its operation as a cooperative venture by villagers may be an increasingly common reaction to its being closed on economic grounds by a big brewery.

In conclusion, it appears that the potential for devising and officially encouraging new forms of community involvement is quite considerable, but that the prospect of a wholesale transfer to 'the community' of functions previously borne by the public sector or by commercial firms must be seen as remote. In so far as rural residents are increasingly urban in their outlook, it appears likely that many will treat with suspicion the idea of departing from a life-style in which all basic needs are considered to be properly the concern of public agencies, commercial firms or the individual household in question. But, of course, changing circumstances might force a reconsideration of this view.

Conclusion

This chapter has attempted to spell out a wide range of policies which might complement, and perhaps reduce the need for, policies directed towards facilitating personal mobility. The emphasis has been on breadth rather than depth and the reader is referred to the UEA study (Moseley. *et al*; 1977) and to the literature cited there for further information on the ideas and schemes reviewed above: it is a field in which innovation is gaining momentum.

Three final points should be made relating to this review of policy options. First, *variety*: the 'toolkit' available to the rural planner for attacking the rural accessibility problem is large and varied. Some of these tools may be little known or even untried. Some may appear useless or else incompatible with the 'old favourites' upon which we have come to depend. Others may seem insufficiently honed or too blunt or unwieldy for the purpose. But they exist and should be thoroughly sorted and appraised before work begins. Second, *context*: none of these options is likely to be universally applicable. Different social, economic, political and geographical conditions conspire to require that solutions be tailor-made for the specific problem in hand. This is not to say that all circumstances are unique and that no general principles can be established with regard either to those circumstances or to the weaknesses and strengths of the various options. The search for such principles is a worthy object of research but it must lead to a better awareness of how policies can be geared to specific contexts. Third, *coordination*: no single agency has a brief to examine and to draw together all of the transport, location and time policies reviewed above. What is more, the various services and activities considered tend to be the responsibility of separate agencies with their own sets of objectives and fields of vision. It may be that many of the most significant advances will come from breaking down these watertight compartments, and the recent (albeit abortive) attempt by the Post Office in Norfolk to deliver newspapers as well as mail is one very small example of this. Individual services may be ripe for integration and the whole 'rural accessibility system' may be ripe for a new attempt at overall coordination.

All of this, the variety and heterogeneity of the policy options, the uniqueness of the contexts within which such options will have to be deployed and the fundamental need for new endeavours in the fields of integration and coordination, points to the necessity to consider the *process of management and coordination* whereby policies should be devised and implemented. This is a major function of the following chapter.

8
Planning and policies: the way ahead

This book is entitled 'Accessibility: the rural *challenge*' and it remains for this final chapter to review that challenge and to suggest how best it might be met. Part of the problem is undoubtedly political: there is not yet sufficiently widespread acceptance that neither rising car ownership nor the gradual relocation of the rural population by migratory movements will ensure levels of accessibility for the whole population which might be termed 'reasonable' by today's standard. Thus part of the challenge lies in developing the political will to attack the rural accessibility problem by continuing and, in certain areas, increasing public intervention in, and financial support of, the relevant systems. The other challenges are technical/managerial. First is a need to develop an organizational context and process of decision-making which will effectively permit the problem to be attacked in a systematic and sustained manner. Second, and given the political will and decision-making context already referred to, is the practical problem concerning just how more services and facilities are to be brought within reasonable access of the carless members of the rural population, drawing upon the whole battery of policy options outlined in the last two chapters. It is these technical/managerial issues that form the focus of this final chapter: the question of political will is omnipresent but it is less clear to the author how this particular requirement can be developed.

The planning process

A basic point is that attempts to improve rural accessibility should respect the fundamentals of the planning process: fragmented *ad hoc* responses to outside stimuli, such as threats that certain bus services will be discontinued, are insufficient. By 'the planning process' is meant an orderly sequence of steps involving: the elucidation of the problem; the setting and weighting of objectives couched in accessibility terms; the formulation of alternative packages of policies; the evaluation of those policy packages in the light of the objectives, cost considerations and the socio-political context; the implementation of the preferred policy package; and, finally, the monitoring both of its success in meeting the objectives and of the continuing applicability of the assumptions upon which it was based.

The heart of this process concerns the formulation and evaluation of alternative policies in the light of accessibility and cost considerations. Here it is important to realize that this inevitably means seeking the best compromise between three incompatible goals:

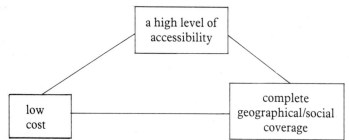

No policy which provides a high level of accessibility throughout a rural area and for all the social groups in need, can be 'low cost'. Similarly, if 'low cost' is the prime consideration then at least one of the other two goals must be sacrificed — in other words the level of accessibility provided must be *either* universal *or* else high for a select few of the rural area's residents. We may term this 'the dilemma of rural accessibility planning' and it will be returned to several times below.

1   ACCESSIBILITY COVERAGE AND STANDARDS

Measuring how far alternative policies might provide accessibility for those in need of it is in essence a simple task, yet in practice it is rarely undertaken. Chapter 4 outlined one way of approaching this task, by means of the accessibility measurement technique used in the UEA study. Doubtless that technique could be improved upon and adapted to specific contexts but it does respect the fundamentals of the planning process outlined above, by permitting the explicit evaluation of alternative policies incorporating locational and transport elements, in terms of the various groups of the community who would be affected. This social, as distinct from geographical, dimension of 'accessibility coverage' is the important one.

Considering the social and geographical 'coverage' that alternative policies imply, should the decision-maker set (or be set) *'standards'* which have to be achieved, or should he be relieved of constraints of this sort? It will be recalled that the evaluation technique described in chapter 4 incorporated something which the research team termed 'standards'. These were simple statements of 'acceptable inconvenience', for example 'access must be possible with a total journey time of under one hour'. Without standards, or rules of thumb of this sort, the evaluation procedure would have been inoperable. Standards in this sense, however, were simply research tools. But there has been a good deal of debate recently concerning the desirability of setting more *fundamental* standards — standards of accessibility which a decision-making body would then commit itself to ensuring.

Standards in this policy sense are well known in other fields. Parker-Morris standards are used, for example, to express minimum levels of housing quality which local authorities must meet in their construction programmes. In the health service, numbers of hospital beds per thousand residents provide a similar contextual element to guide decision-making. But in the field of accessibility, such standards are rare. The provisions of the 1944 Education Act concerning the right of children to get to school at the education authority's expense, if they live more than three miles away, provide an isolated example of a 'national accessibility standard'.

It is not difficult to see why such standards are so rare. Being mandatory by nature, they would imply considerable programmes of expenditure in the remoter rural areas where high levels of access are so much more costly to provide. And of course they also deny any *local* assessment of priorities: the local role becomes one of implementation at least cost. But while certain accessibility agencies, for example, Oxfordshire County Council (Ennor, 1976), shun the expression of even county-wide (much less nation-wide) accessibility standards on the grounds that they would stifle local (in the Oxfordshire case, district and parish) initiative, others are beginning to define such standards, if only to give themselves something to aim at.

Such standards can be genuinely county-wide. Cheshire County Council, for example (Lea and Archibald, 1976), has declared that *all* of its villages should be within one mile of a public transport service which gives:

(i) one return trip per weekday to a primary and a secondary school;

(ii) one return trip per week to a centre with a specified range of shops and other services;

(iii) a connection with a service giving one trip per week to any hospital in the area.

More frequently, however, and respecting the incompatability of 'universality' and 'quality' when it comes to setting accessibility standards (the basic 'dilemma of rural accessibility planning' referred to above), a number of county councils are beginning to establish standards which vary spatially. As a result of its study of the northwest area of the county, the Bedfordshire County Council (1975), for example, established the following standards as a basis for developing policies incorporating the diversion of scheduled buses, the use of postbuses, and the use of schoolbuses by adult passengers:

Settlement size

50 inhabitants	. . .	once-weekly shopping service
100 "	. . .	daily journey to work service
200 "	. . .	guaranteed access to a doctor's surgery
500 "	. . .	a daily shopping service, a once-weekly return service after 10 pm and a Sunday service

Another way of reaching a reasonable trade-off between universality and quality of service would be to express standards in terms of service frequencies. One could envisage, for example, the matrices drawn up by the Association of Transport Coordinating Officers and portrayed in table 3.1 being divided

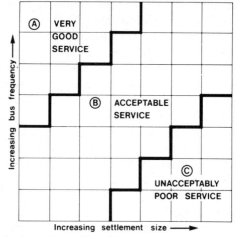

Figure 8.1 Settlement size and bus frequency as parameters in
accessibility standards
(Note: This figure should be examined in conjunction with Table 3.1)

into three portions as in figure 8.1. In this latter figure, which
again plots service quality (vertical axis) by settlement size, area 'B'
denotes an acceptable level of services which constitute a standard
to which settlements in category 'C' should be raised — if necessary by diverting resources from the more lavishly served category
'A' settlements. (However, it should be remembered that the
central argument of this book is that the intrinsic quality of bus
services, expressed here in terms of 'frequency per week', is much
less useful a parameter than are measures of the access to activities
that such services afford. The vertical axis might therefore be
redefined in accessibility, rather than mobility, terms.)

The general point is that the use of accessibility standards
provides a valuable way into 'the dilemma of rural accessibility
planning'. It is an attractive alternative to the approach which puts
a cost-constraint in prime position — for example, a ceiling of
£250,000 per annum on subsidy payments to the bus operators, or
a statement that the county council will only (and always) subsidize
a bus service if it meets a fixed proportion of its operating costs.
The most sensible thing is surely to experiment, at the planning
stage, with a range of alternative combinations of cost, level of
access and socio-geographical coverage.

On balance, then, the author agrees with the conclusion of the Association of Transport Coordinating Officers (1976) — that no attempt should be made by the government to impose national minimum accessibility standards. In order to apply equally to Surrey and to Cumbria they would have either to be uselessly low or else involve a transfer of resources from the urban and suburban to the rural areas, which few people would think equitable. A much more useful and practicable role for central government would be for it to *require* county councils to establish, use and publicize their *own* accessibility standards, witholding its financial support until these were adequately undertaken. These standards would then play a central role in the formulation of the rural elements of the council's transport and spatial plans, and be made quite clear to the residents and would-be residents of the various parts of the county. In other words, central government should strongly encourage county councils to be socially aware in this respect, by means of its Transport Supplementary Grant payments and other sanctions, but it should not attempt to prescribe the standards itself.

2 COSTS

The essence of the argument against the imposition of national accessibility standards is that 'accessibility at any price' can prove grossly extravagant: the third element of the trilogy of factors comprising the 'dilemma of rural accessibility planning' (namely accessibility-coverage-cost) must receive proper consideration. Both the scale of expenditure and its incidence are important.

Chapter 5 stressed the wide range of relevant costs. Not only should the analysis include capital and current, and public and private-sector costs, but also those incurred both within and outside the transport sector. The costs of retaining (or re-establishing) small village schools and 'uneconomic' village post offices should properly be considered along with those of running, or subsidizing, schools transport and stage bus services. This will rarely be a simple task: in the UEA study, for example, it was found to be quite impossible to ascertain the cost to the Post Office Corporation of its retaining small rural post offices — the financial data are apparently not tabulated in an appropriate format.

In the more narrowly defined field of public transport costing there are of course two basic tasks: first, an estimation of the *gross* costs which would be incurred by running a hypothetical service, and second an estimation of the revenue through fare payments which might be expected, and thereby of *net* costs (or profit). This is, understandably, a field well known to transport economists and operators. Suffice it to say that models estimating the gross, or operating, costs of possible services generally incorporate at least three elements: the time duration of the service, which largely determines the labour cost; its mileage, to which are related fuel consumption and vehicle wear and tear; and the service's requirement for vehicles in peak-hour periods, the last mentioned in large part determining the total vehicle stock of the company.

Revenue (and, thereby, *net* cost) estimates must be build upon forecasts of behaviour: will people actually *use* such a service if it is provided? There are two possible approaches. The first approach is to attempt to model behaviour, based on real-world observations, with trip-making being expressed as a function of demographic factors, fare-levels, service frequency, etc. The problem here is that in rural areas present behaviour is so constrained by the poor and patchy nature of public transport that a model developed in such a context might be quite inappropriate in circumstances of more generous provision (a problem already referred to in chapter 4). The second approach is to rely on a household survey of possible users. But however sophisticated such a survey, it generally rests on some formulation of the 'would you use a bus service if..?' type of question. Unfortunately respondents are notoriously ready to over-estimate their likely use of hypothetical services for a variety of reasons. By replying 'yes' they may see themselves as keeping their travel options open, helping their neighbours and visitors, and perhaps also improving the value of their house. The problem is that many bus operators have been disappointed by the poor actual use of a service provided on the basis of such market research, with the service being subsequently withdrawn after an experimental period. A more promising approach is probably to seek to establish 'frustrated movement' by examining the actual trip-making behaviour of carless individuals, against a yardstick of the behaviour of similar individuals who do have a car.

But whatever the method actually used for estimating net costs the crucial thing is for the decision-making process to recognize their relative size in the context of all the other public sector costs involved. As chapter 5 demonstrated, the latter will often be much greater, if less obvious.

3 IMPLEMENTATION

Finally, potential transport and spatial systems should be evaluated not only in terms of the scale and incidence of the accessibility benefits and the costs which they imply, but also in terms of the problems of implementation which may be involved. Two points should be made here. First, does the planning body actually 'control the levers' which will put the policy into action? If the answer is, as it almost certainly will be 'only to a certain extent', then what guarantee is there that the other agencies concerned will play their part? Not only does this realization of limited potency necessitate close coordination with these other agencies (on which, see pp. 103-6) but it also requires a sanguine look at the roles, potential, and powers of 'the community'. Policies built upon public involvement in car-sharing schemes or in other community transport schemes, must include some provision for ensuring that such support will be forthcoming and/or a fall-back contingency plan should expectations prove unsubstantiated.

The second point relates to the timing and reversibility of the proposed policy. It is important not only to ask how quickly and easily a policy might be implemented, but also to consider the speed and ease with which it might be discontinued if circumstances change. Considerations both of speed of implementation and of reversibility tend to favour transport-type policies rather than location-type policies, particularly if the latter involve heavy and long-term programmes of investment. But while it follows that the problems of old people getting to a post office cannot be dismissed with an assurance that once the structure plan is implemented most carless elderly people will live close to rural post offices, this does not itself invalidate the need for locational policies which gradually reduce the problem of isolation.

Given all the problems of predicting, in the planning office, the benefits, costs and difficulties of implementing alternative hypothetical policies, it becomes tempting to call instead for reliance on real-world experimental schemes whose performance would be carefully monitored (such as those described at the end of chapter 6). In this way, the argument runs, these various criteria of performance may be actually measured rather than guessed at. But while of course there must be experiments and pilot schemes if real-world difficulties are to be appreciated and taken account of in future policies, such schemes cannot take the place of careful 'desk work' of the sort described in this section. Real-world experiments must, by their very nature, involve specific routes, timings, fare-levels, operating conditions, etc. It is with the hypothetical *variation* of factors such as these that the process of accessibility planning is essentially concerned — and given both the timelag of public response to service alterations and the operational difficulties of carrying out frequent modifications, then much of this work must necessarily be reserved for the albeit artificial conditions of 'the laboratory'. Running experimental services must be seen as just one part — and often an expensive part — of this wider research process.

4 COORDINATION AND PUBLIC INVOLVEMENT

The comprehensive process of accessibility planning described above can only really be achieved if the various agencies with executive power work more closely together. Chapter 5 has already established that a wide range of bodies affect the *ability* of rural residents to travel, and that an even larger number affect their *need* to travel by influencing the location of service outlets. It also established the substantial public sector resources involved — a sum very much greater than mere public transport subsidies. Advances have been made in the coordination of public transport provision in rural areas, particularly following the duties imposed upon county councils by Section 203 of the 1972 Local Government Act and the subsequent preparation of Transport Policies and Programmes which are intended to look broadly at the needs and potential of various modes of transport in each county. And most county councils now employ at least one officer in a transport coordinating role, albeit often with a much narrower remit than the one implicit in the previous section.

What practical steps can be taken to foster a more coordinated approach to relevant decision-making by the following agencies: county council (including its constituent planning, education, surveyor's and social services departments), district council, Post Office Corporation, Regional/Area Health Authority, National Bus Company subsidiaries, British Rail, the Traffic Commissioners, the Departments of Environment and Transport, the independent bus operators and other private firms? It seems clear that improved coordination should build upon the powers and responsibilities currently enjoyed by the county councils, which have the central spatial planning and transport coordinating roles in rural areas, have major executive responsibilities in schools transport, road construction and maintenance and bus service subsidy, and which are thereby most intimately linked with the other agencies. A number of suggestions will therefore be put forward in this vein. (The reader should also note the postscript to this chapter, concerned with the 1978 Transport Bill's proposal that 'county public transport plans' be drawn up.)

For the reasons already advanced in chapter 5 the county councils should be much more closely involved in route licensing. At the very least the Traffic Commissioners should be required to pay more attention to the county councils' expressed objectives and policies, when considering applications for new or modified services. More ambitiously, route licensing could be made a *joint* responsibility of the Traffic Commissioners and county councils. The former would have regard to the implementation of national policies, to regional or intercounty matters and to the operators' need for a reasonably stable environment. The latter would have regard to the implementation of its transportation and land-use strategies and to the achievement of reasonable standards of accessibility for the various parts of the county and groups in the community.

A second need is for the closer integration of both structure and local planning with the preparation of Transport Policies and Programmes. The Department of the Environment in its circulars 104/73 and 98/74, dealing with local transport grants and structure plans respectively, has urged the drawing together of county transport planning and county land-use planning into a common process. But there seems to be a clear difference between the integration of the various elements of accessibility planning which is *permitted* by the relevant legislation and that which actually *occurs*. Perhaps central government (the Department of Environment or of Transport, as appropriate) could do more to foster such integration by requiring in TPP and structure plan submissions a more thorough approach to the examination of needs and of resources in the accessibility field (along the lines set out above) — including an unequivocal statement of the accessibility objectives or standards being pursued and a justification of the policies selected to attain them. A brief description in these submissions of the various attempts made by the county council to liaise with the various agencies listed above might also be useful.

In short, the county councils should be given a clearer 'accessibility planning' function. The various Transport Coordinating Officers employed by the councils generally have only very limited resources of staff at their disposal, and often they have only been in the post for a short period. And practice varies greatly from county to county. But it is still fair to say that their work tends to be passive and piecemeal in that they tend to respond to proposed service modifications and to try to coordinate timetables rather than to devise and implement a comprehensive strategy. Also it is a narrow role that they play: the location and hours of availability of the activities to which access is needed, as well as certain transport services such as schools transport and mobile libraries, generally fall outside their area of responsibility. And their attempts at coordination tend to be much more concerned with modes of transport than with executive agencies. In short there is a clear need for a shift from 'transport' to 'accessibility' and from 'coordination' to 'planning and management'. Just how a shift in this direction might best be achieved in practice will depend on the particular departmental structure and decision-making processes of each county council.

Whatever the precise organizational context adopted, this 'accessibility planning and management' function could probably best be undertaken in the context of systematic reviews of the total accessibility situation within constituent parts of the county.

From these reviews would come proposals which would be embodied in timetable revisions, TPP submissions, structure plan revisions, and the sectoral policies of other agencies. These accessibility reviews would reduce the duplication involved in individual agencies undertaking their own surveys of transport and service provision and needs (for example the market research work of NBC subsidiaries, and the surveys of transport needs undertaken by the various county council departments and by the health authorities). Information would be communally gathered and pooled. In most counties, these reviews would be most conveniently undertaken for areas no larger and probably smaller, than the constituent district council areas (or the geographical 'sectors' used by Eastern Counties Omnibus Co. in its rolling programme of timetable revisions). The experience of ECOC (whose exercises, though involving quite extensive household surveys are of course much narrower than those envisaged) and that of the UEA research team which surveyed and proposed policies for two case study areas in Norfolk, suggests that six months is the minimum for a proper planning exercise involving adequate research and public consultation. And so if, for example, the rural parts of a county were divided into six areas the programme might be completed in three years and then recommenced (see figure 8.2). The very cooperation between agencies needed to execute such a comprehensive area-based accessibility planning exercise would itself be likely to bear fruit in the form of cooperation between them in service provision.

The accessibility planning exercise described above should involve genuine *public participation* both through sample household, and possible on-vehicle, surveys and through the careful questioning of those active in the community such as parish clerks and councillors, clergymen and voluntary social workers. There seems to be no valid reason why public participation is statutory for structure planning but not for transport planning (or indeed for education, health service and other forms of public planning). Indeed the disappointing experience of many public participation exercises on structure planning issues, would be unlikely to be replicated in the proposed area accessibility studies which would relate to more clearly relevant, local and 'concrete' matters. In short, local involvement in accessibility planning is essential and the

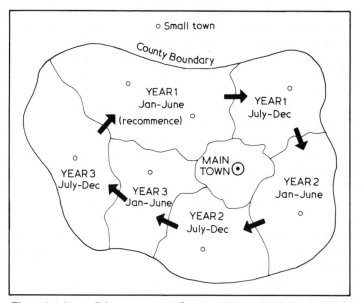

Figure 8.2 A possible programme for area-wide accessibility planning

participation exercise would be designed to provide views upon local needs and problems, possible policies which might otherwise be overlooked, and the feasibility of alternative policies from the point of view of public acceptability and involvement.

But how far is it possible to go beyond involving the public in determining the services to be provided and to involve them also in actually providing those services? Chapter 7 has already reviewed the difficulties of community involvement in this field. But certain constraints could and should be relaxed. The effect of route licensing restrictions upon innovation has already been discussed in chapter 6 (and the 1978 Transport Bill promises some relief here — see the postscript). Another major constraint is the deficiency of 'leadership' and entrepreneurial flair in many villages. Often there seems to be an inverse correlation between a rural community's need for mutual assistance, and its ability to provide it. Villages worst off in terms of public transport and service provision tend also to be poorest in community resources: either they have small populations or they have a preponderance of elderly or low-income households.

Perhaps this particular constraint could be relaxed in part by a policy of providing community workers or 'catalysts' for a carefully selected group of rural parishes, particularly those in the more remote areas. Their job would primarily be to generate public involvement in schemes such as the following: an introduction service for those offering and seeking lifts by car; a parents' 'taxi' service for the school journeys of their neighbours' children as well as their own; a residents' transport club for shopping and leisure outings and organized, perhaps, on a subscription basis; a community bus scheme; a car-sharing scheme for specific activities such as hospital visiting; the operation of the village pub on a cooperative basis.

But these 'catalysts' could also profitably liaise with higher authorities — as a reference point in a two-way flow of information between council and constituent, as a channel of pressure for a bus route diversion or the provision of a postbus and as a significant part of the area-wide accessibility planning process described above. In short, as well as their catalyst role they would have a clear monitoring role involving them in keeping an eye on problems and policies as they develop and in passing on complaints and suggestions to the relevant bodies, particularly in the bi/triennial accessibility review. Such 'rural community catalysts' would, then, play a role not unlike that of the 'parish journeymen' organized by certain west country Rural Community Councils, the more energetic secretaries of community health councils, or the community workers advocated by some of the Community Development Projects. It is unlikely that volunteers could be relied upon to do a job demanding both in time and in managerial skills. But even if these catalysts were salaried local government officers (with a large degree of independence guaranteed) and even if a small pump-priming fund were placed at their disposal, such an approach could well prove to be economically very sensible in the context of the social problems described and of the alternative ways in which money relevant to personal accessibility is presently being spent.

Policy proposals

So far we have been concerned with the *process* whereby policies appropriate to a given context might best be devised and implemented. Such an emphasis reflects the belief that there are no panaceas and that packages of policies must be tailormade for the problem in hand. But it would be wrong to conclude a review of the challenge of rural accessibility planning without some indication of the relative merits of the items on the 'shopping list' of options outlined in chapters 6 and 7. Which of those options should properly come high on the list of possibilities, and what shape might the eventual overall strategy for an area take?

1 INDIVIDUAL POLICY ELEMENTS

Following the convention established earlier, these elements will be considered under three headings: location, transport/communications and time. (The reader is referred to chapters 6 and 7 for the evidence upon which the following conclusions are based.)

(i) *Location policies*

The principal locational issue concerns whether the present tendency for many small-village activities to close and for 'key villages' or service centres to develop, should be resisted or encouraged. The principal village activities which are relevant comprise three in the public sector, namely primary schools, village halls and post offices, and two in the private sector — village shops and pubs.

In the case of *village shops* it appears that their viability varies not just with the size of their market but with less tangible qualities relating to the proprietor. Local authorities could consider providing indirect assistance to village shops by means of some form of differential rating and by attempting to restrain new development in competing centres. In addition, local authorities should be empowered to subsidize small shops and to undertake municipal trading, since in essence there is little difference between the state's subsidy or provision of transport to an activity and its removing the need to use such transport. In practice the awarding of selective subsidies to shops would be an invidious and difficult process and would probably be of limited value in most cases. Further, taking over village shops and running them at a loss could involve not only an open-ended commitment but also the erosion of the small businessman's local involvement with the community. But there could be a careful contractual arrangement in which the subsidy was clearly limited and made conditional upon pricing, range of stock and other factors, or else be linked with a requirement to operate an ancillary service such as a sub-post office. There is no convincing reason why the *option* of subsidizing or operating shops should not be permitted.

As for *village schools*, the view that they should all be retained at any cost is untenable in any reasoned consideration of the deployment of resources. The returns to scale in primary school provision increase rapidly at least up to a size of about 50-70 pupils — but probably not thereafter. The savings involved in a modest degree of spatial concentration would in counties such as Norfolk more than offset the costs of transporting pupils to larger schools. But this ignores the social and educational advantages that are sometimes claimed for small rural schools, and these *may* be substantial.

Regarding *pubs and post offices*, very little information on the supply side seems to be available. Indeed this suggests a general conclusion: that an explicit period of notice be given to the local authority of any impending closure of a village commercial activity — at least in designated 'low access zones' (defined below) — so that the local subsidy or operation of that activity might at least be considered.

A further recommendation is that local authorities consider the possibility of designating and financially supporting a 'village activist' — a person who may already be providing one service, for example a village shop, and who would be prepared to provide accommodation and publicity for other services which would visit the village on an itinerant basis, such as a mobile chiropody or post office service.

Key village policies involving the deliberate spatial concentration of service outlets have much to commend them, if they are accompanied by appropriate housing and transport policies. Deliberate spatial concentration, at the local inter-village level (whether of related activities, for example the grouping of a doctor, dentist and chemist in a health centre, or of unrelated activities, for example post office, chemist, hardware store) confers a number of benefits upon the carless. First, it reduces the diffuse pattern of local trips and thereby makes more possible a locally focused public transport service of some sort. Second, it extends to them the scope for multi-purpose shopping/service trips long enjoyed by the car-borne. Third, it permits a generally higher level and wider choice of services to be made available to them than would a policy of 'scatter'. But on grounds of equity a key village policy must be accompanied (and in examining structure plan submissions the Department of Environment should satisfy itself on this) by appropriate complementary policies relating to the areas *not* selected for preferential treatment.

(ii) *Transport and communication policies*

Two introductory points should be made before we consider individual transport modes. First, transport policies are particularly important in accessibility planning because, to the extent that they are not capital intensive, they can be introduced and if necessary discontinued, quite quickly. They provide the speed and flexibility that location policies lack. Second, individual transport elements should in practice not be considered in isolation. They should be appraised for their suitability in forming part of an overall strategy: some might be useful chiefly in providing feeder services of a local nature, others in providing off-peak services complementary to the main provision of transport at peak periods, and so on.

The conventional bus (41 seats or over) will probably and properly remain the main form of non-car-based mechanized personal transport in rural areas, in the foreseeable future. Stage carriage bus services are likely to, and should, continue to play the central role in public transport between the large villages and small towns of rural areas. Indeed, even in more local rural transport, of a feeder nature, the conventional bus will frequently constitute the best mode of transport. There are two reasons for this. First, work and school peak-hour flows are likely to continue to require large and numerous vehicles, the off-peak marginal costs of which are sufficiently low for them to compete favourably with smaller vehicles purchased principally for the off-peak period. Second, smaller vehicles do not give pro rata cuts in operating costs because labour costs, and to a lesser extent administration costs, loom large. And removing labour and administration costs by relying on voluntary systems is likely to be a realistic option only in especially favourable circumstances.

Thus, it is suggested that improving the use of the existing bus fleet can bring about more significant results in many circumstances than would the introduction of unconventional transport. This is likely to mean a programme of modifying the routeing and timing of present services, either on a minor scale, for example by allowing diversions from the main route on a selective demand-actuated basis, or on a major scale as in the periodic total re-examination of the small area network as advocated above. It also implies a need for a rigorous examination of the potential for a more intensive use of the existing fleet outside 'peak' and 'unsocial' hours. For example, the county's Transport Coordinating Officer, or a 'rural community catalyst', could promote a once-weekly shoppers' bus financed, perhaps, by the traders who would benefit, or a 'bus club' arrangement whereby villagers charter a manned bus for regular shopping and, possibly, entertainment trips.

As for the *operation* of conventional buses in rural areas, the NBC subsidiaries appear generally most suited for providing a basic scheduled transport network linking the major villages with each other and with the urban centres. Where such services are not commercially viable, the county councils will have to fulfil a contractual role, indicating the routes and timings required, and paying the appropriate subsidies. The independent bus operators should be encouraged to play a valuable role in complementing this basic pattern of service provision. Often they enjoy certain economies when compared with the NBC subsidiaries. But, being typically small in size, individualist in style and governed by the profit motive, there may be problems in shaping their contribution towards the achievement of accessibility standards.

Rail services, where they remain in rural areas, can provide valuable links with large urban centres and with the inter-city rail network. A number of the hypothetical strategies developed and evaluated for a part of Norfolk, in the UEA study, built upon an improved bus-rail interchange in the small town of North Walsham with significant improvements in accessibility resulting. In addition, two forms of rail utilization which may often be worthwhile and are relatively easy to implement are the selective re-opening of closed stations or the construction of unstaffed halts, and the improvement of bus-rail interchanges so as to reduce wasteful duplication and to cut overall passenger journey times.

So much for conventional bus and rail transport. If we consider *unconventional modes* (namely those which either employ small vehicles or rely on voluntary involvement or both) then most of the schemes reviewed in chapter 6 are likely to have a useful role in specific circumstances — some more than others. But excessive enthusiasm for the unconventional should be tempered by the high labour and administration costs of many schemes, by the localized incidence of volunteer enthusiasm and skills, and by the frequent conflict between accessibility objectives and others pursued by the relevant agencies.

The main attraction of the *postbus* is that it requires neither voluntary labour nor total reliance on the paying passenger to justify its commercial operation. Such a dual purpose ('freight' and passengers) service has much to commend it, since the marginal cost of carrying passengers is usually very small. But postbuses are limited severely by their circuitous routes, which necessitate slow overall speeds, and by their inconvenient timing. However, it is possible that such disadvantages could be reduced with some slight loss in operating efficiency and, perhaps, some considerable increase in personal accessibility opportunities. Put differently, it is reasonable to ask whether rural residents might willingly trade-off a deterioration in the timing and frequency of postal deliveries and collections in their area for an improvement in the public transport available to them. The Post Office Corporation appears to have shown great willingness to operate postbuses if their routes and timings (with only small modifications) are acceptable to the county councils and if the latter pick up the bill for any deficit. The latter requirement seems reasonable, but the POC should be permitted, perhaps required, to be much more flexible — even to sacrifice its own postal standards — if the county council requests and is prepared to underwrite timing and routeing modifications.

Considering *the schoolbus* the central issue is again the conflict between the objectives of broadly based accessibility planning and those of a narrowly conceived service. Even accepting that going to school is the only personal trip required by law, and that without subsidized provision this trip would often be very difficult to make, we must ask whether the 'minimum accessibility standards' laid down in the 1944 Education Act still constitute an appropriate 'pre-emptive strike' when the time comes to take a total view of an area's accessibility requirements. Even if there must remain a mandatory duty on parents to send their children to school, should there remain a mandatory duty on society to provide the transport to permit that duty to be exercised, irrespective of where the parents choose to live? The point simply is that educational transport should not remain an isolated sector of expenditure, divorced from the mainstream of county accessibility planning. The scope for carrying fare-paying adults on 'school buses' is very limited at present because most are already close to capacity. But in many rural areas the child population will fall in the future and some spare capacity should result. County councils should be encouraged (they are already empowered) to allow the carrying of some adult passengers if only by prior arrangement and in otherwise busless parishes.

'*Dial-a-ride*' schemes (as practiced in urban and suburban areas) are very unlikely to prove of value in the rural context. Their high cost per passenger carried characteristic would be accentuated by the scattered distribution of population in precisely those rural areas — away from the main settlements and lines of communication — where their value in social terms might be greatest. The fact that most carless rural households also lack a telephone only underlines the unsuitability of rural dial-a-ride. But this is not to damn completely the introduction of a demand-actuation element into certain transport services. Three possible schemes might be suggested: first, the selective diversion of conventional buses on a 'drop me off' basis, or even on a 'pick up' basis if this could be inexpensively arranged and if the resultant unpredictability did not undermine the necessary coordination of different services; second, a minibus service running to a notional timetable, with selective diversions to collect passengers who have placed an order by telephone, by letter or by a prior message to the driver; third, a health service minibus collecting patients with appointments at a doctor's surgery or at a health centre, and out-patients and visitors who need to get to a certain hospital.

Voluntary transport schemes involving unpaid drivers have obvious economic attractions. '*Car sharing*', in which lifts are offered and accepted on an organized basis, can fall foul of problems of indebtedness and of incongruent life-styles, even if payment is allowed. But this is not to say that it should not be permitted and encouraged in the most poorly serviced areas where the relaxation of the route licensing constraint would lead to only a negligible amount of traffic being abstracted from conventional transport services. Fostering such schemes could be a major responsibility of the 'rural community catalyst'. Similarly *community bus* schemes, along the lines of the pioneer service run in North Norfolk, should be encouraged, again in the remoter areas and perhaps with the county councils providing entrepreneurial support.

In contrast, innovations in *telecommunications* are unlikely to offer much in the foreseeable future. For most of the activities with which we are principally concerned — work, shopping, education, medicine and leisure — information provision *complements* and does not obviate the need for personal movement by either 'client' or 'supplier'. Each activity generally requires face-to-face contact at some stage and the *combined* cost of subsidizing the universal installation and operation even of telephones *and* of subsidizing the associated transport services to take the activity to the person or vice versa, would probably be prohibitive. And, of course, shopping and other face-to-face contacts have a considerable social value for many of the disadvantaged, isolated groups with whom we are principally concerned.

(iii) *Time policies*

Policies which involve the retiming of activities or affect the 'time-budgets' of people should be considered in the same analytical framework as location and transport policies. Like transport policies they are attractive in terms of their potential for quick and reversible implementation. Like both transport and locational policies they relate to activities at present in both private and public-sector hands. Four suggestions can be made:

(a) The increased synchronization of off-peak activities requiring full-time attendance by different clientele (e.g., bingo, evening classes and cinema, synchronized at the same time on the same days). This 'temporal clustering' presupposes of course the 'spatial clustering' of the relevant activities and adds extra weight to our general support of location policies which build upon key villages and small towns.

(b) The reduced synchronization of activities requiring peak-hour movement, so that the costs involved in maintaining a vehicle fleet and labour force sufficient to meet peak hour travel, are reduced. (This may not *always* be the right policy: if the peak is light, then increased synchronization might enhance the viability of a public transport service.) Flexible working hours and staggered school hours offer the greatest possibilities. But it should be remembered that such changes will indirectly affect the time-budgets or *other* people, for example mothers having to stay at home later or return home earlier so as to accommodate their children's school hours, and therefore need to be carefully research.

(c) The extending of the opening hours of activities of a 'drop-in' (rather than long, continuous attendance) nature. Evening shopping, Saturday banking and Saturday attendance at local government offices all provide examples of the possibilities, though implementation would be difficult in many cases.

(d) The coordination of public-sector peripatetic services so that they congregate on a single weekday in each of a sequence of large villages. These villages, on these particular days, would be the focus of some form of community minibus scheme, serving adjacent areas, the vehicle being 'handed on' from day to day and from zone to zone. This scheme would effectively translate to the village scale and to the public sector, the rotation between small towns of private sector retailers on a weekly market basis. It was described in more detail in chapter 7 and provides a possible way of bringing near to the rural resident's home such services as the citizen's advice bureau, post office, family planning clinic, dentist, etc. Coordination in the time, location and transport dimensions provides the key to ensuring the ability of the carless to make multi-purpose trips.

2 THE AREA-WIDE STRATEGY

The various policy elements reviewed briefly above, and at greater length in chapters 6 and 7, must be welded into an area-wide strategy, and the earlier part of this chapter outlined a planning process by means of which this might be done. In essence, the problem is to find for a given area the best trade-off of the three elements comprising the 'dilemma of rural accessibility planning' — low cost, high accessibility and complete socio-geographical coverage.

This welding together of individual elements should not, of course, be purely in the spatial dimension. Figure 8.3 sets out a hypothetical daily pattern of services between a rural settlement and a neighbouring town. (This diagram can profitably be examined alongside figure 4.6 which describes the time-space realm of a hypothetical rural housewife.) It suggests, for example, the possibility of a housewife making a trip to town by postbus in the early afternoon, returning by 'schoolbus' or 'work's bus' later in the day. The point, simply, is that the eventual strategy must be three-dimensional, with the individual elements of policy being fitted together in both time and space.

When we focus on the spatial dimensions of the sort of area-wide strategy which is likely to emerge from the planning process outlined earlier, the central point is that an explicitly hierarchical pattern of provision is virtually bound to emerge. Servicing remoter areas implies higher per capita costs and this in turn means that lower standards of provision in those areas must generally be accepted as inevitable. Precise evidence on costs is hard to acquire but plotting public sector, per capita costs of 'accessibility provision' against a cumulative measure of the population served, is likely to give curves like those described in figure 8.4. Different standards of service (using 'standards' to mean measures of service quality) will give different absolute cost figures: compare the three curves in the diagram. But the gently, then quickly, rising shape of the curves is probably common to each. The bulk of the population — those living in towns, large villages and on the interconnecting routes — can be assured a certain level of service fairly cheaply. But the last few per cent of the population — living in isolated dwellings or small hamlets — imply a disproportionate level of expenditure. It

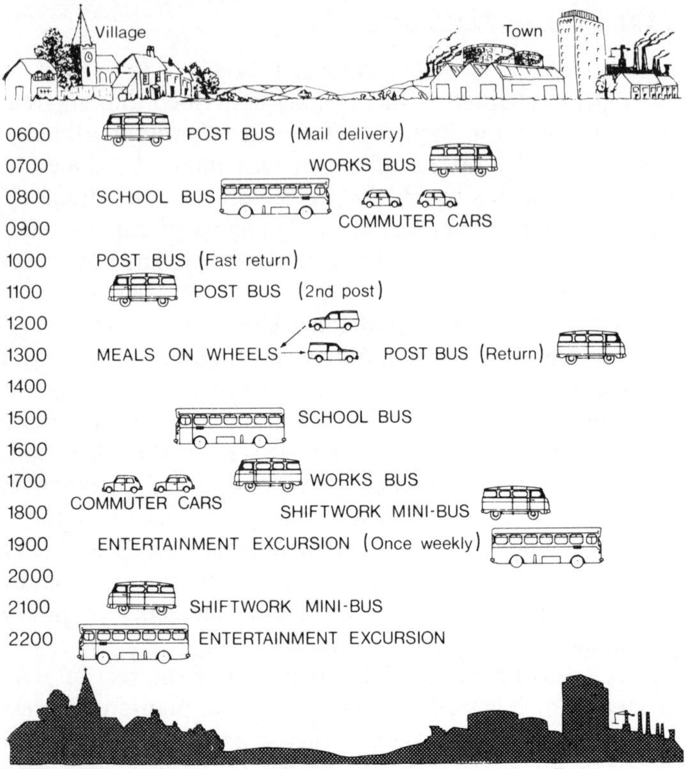

Figure 8.3 A daily pattern of transport movements between village and town

seems inevitable, and basically equitable, that a strategy involving the differential treatment of people living in areas of differing remoteness, be pursued. This could take the form of the ABC strategy in figure 8.4

In short, an explicitly hierarchical land-use/transport strategy is, in the author's opinion, both desirable and inevitable in a cost-conscious climate. Such a strategy would formally integrate the hierarchical settlement system embodied in most structure plans, with a hierarchical arrangement of public transport routes. The latter would comprise:

(1) *A basic inter-town network* of conventional buses or, occasionally, of rail links. This would incorporate many (but not all) of the key villages and be on a limited-stop basis. Not all

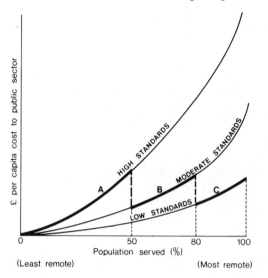

Figure 8.4 The public sector costs of meeting alternative accessibility standards in rural areas

adjacent pairs of small towns need be connected: those which effectively duplicate each other's function would not normally warrant a direct link.

(2) *A local network of 'rural routes'*, generally focused on a small town where most activities would be located and where connections could be easily made with the inter-town network. The experimental work undertaken in the UEA study suggested that circular routes might often prove most attractive in accessibility terms. Many of the rural routes would be serviced by conventional buses: other would rely on unconventional transport.

Associated with the hierarchical transport/land-use plan, a clear categorization of areas and settlements is advocated, in terms of the accessibility standards they would enjoy. Figure 8.5 indicates what a three-tier accessibility pattern might look like in practice, with the small town and favoured villages at limited-stop points on the inter-urban network enjoying a set of *high* accessibility standards; most of the other key villages, and the corridors joining them, enjoying *medium* accessibility standards; and the rest of the area (the 'low access zones') having only *minimum*

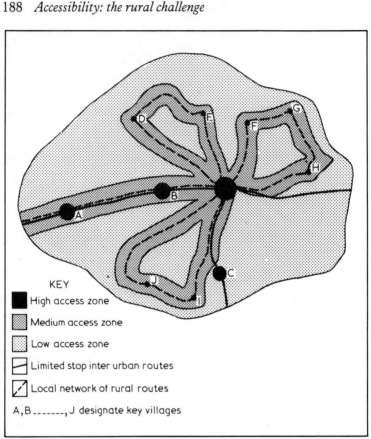

Figure 8.5 A three-tier, small area accessibility strategy

standards. Obviously, the accessibility planner should try to get as many rural residents as possible in the 'high' or, failing that, the 'medium' access zones. Also, a feature of such a strategy would be good inter-change facilities, with suitable facilities for waiting at the points of interconnection, carefully timetabled connections, through-fare tickets, etc.

But '*low access zones*', with only minimal standards of assured accessibility, will exist. Indeed they *already* exist in all county planning and transport strategies, and in one sense the only novelty about the proposed strategy is its insistence that the existence, extent and nature of such zones be recognized *explicitly and overtly* rather than *implicitly and covertly*. And given their inevitable existence they should be the subject of a package of policies as clear and open as those applied to the more favoured areas. These policies should be designed to relieve the hardship implied by the absence of conventional public transport and the paucity of other services. In short, while *spatial* discrimination in favour of the best-served areas is to some degree inevitable, complementary policies discriminating in favour of disadvantaged *social* groups should be followed in the 'low access zones'.

Many of these 'low access zone' policies have already been outlined. They include: the appointment of rural community catalysts; the relaxation of route licensing restrictions so that community-based transport schemes can more easily operate; a housing policy designed to give the residents of low access areas a real chance of moving to better served areas; encouraging the Post Office Corporation to relax its postal objectives in favour of certain passenger transport objectives; the selective support of retail and other services in danger of closure; fostering the dissemination of information to carless residents; allowing adults to make selective use of schools transport.

Many of these suggestions might be equally useful outside the designated 'low access zones'. But the point is simply that they should be devised and publicised as an explicit package of policies for those areas. Existing residents and would-be residents would then know clearly what to expect and what is expected of them. Some of the suggestions, relating for example to the Post Office being enabled to pursue 'non-Post Office' objectives and to the relaxation of route licensing in designated areas, would probably require legislation. But taking a longer term view this should not be insuperable.

This takes the discussion as far as is possible in suggesting policy elements and area-wide strategies which might be of value in different parts of the country. The theme throughout has been that the formulation of policy should be a matter of *local* concern, and it is partly for this reason that so much emphasis has been placed on the decision-making process and the organizational context within which that process might best operate. The essence of the approach is that a broad view should be taken of the resources and policy options available, and a clear view taken of the objectives to be achieved. Most important, the *incidence* of benefits, both socially and spatially, should be made explicit and made the subject of informed debate. In short, rural accessibility planning must now specify clearly where it is going, why it is going there and how it intends to make the trip.

Postscript: The 1978 Transport Bill, and beyond

Consideration of the 1978 Transport Bill has not been incorporated into the preceding text because of its, as yet, undefinitive status. But certain of its intended provisions should be briefly described at this stage.

An earlier government White Paper (Department of Transport, 1977) which argued the need for increased local involvement in transport planning foreshadowed many of these provisions. With regard specifically to rural areas, the White Paper stressed that 'the maintenance of an effective network of bus services in the country is an important aim of the government's transport policy', and it went on to say that 'bus services need finance, basic stability and imaginative development. The government aims to provide the first two and to secure the right conditions for the third.' The Bill's principal provision for ensuring adequate finance and stability for rural transport relates to its requirement that non-metropolitan county councils prepare and publish *county public transport plans*. (The government had previously admitted (Department of Transport, circular 3/78) that 'in general the TPP's are still a disappointing record of the transport planning being carried out in the counties'.) These new plans, though produced annually, should look five years ahead, review existing services in relation to need and show how the county council intends to carry out its duty of promoting a coordinated and efficient system of public transport to meet the needs of the county. An important element of the plans will be the agreements, normally of three years' duration, that the councils will enter into with public passenger transport undertakings to provide financial support for services which would not otherwise be provided. A further welcome development is that the Traffic Commissioners will be required to take such plans into consideration in exercising their road service licensing functions.

A second important part of the Bill relates to public service vehicle licensing. The proposal is that, if certain conditions are fulfilled, vehicles carrying no more than seven passengers will be completely exempt from road service licensing. In other words, the new legislation will remove the legal obstacles to car-sharing, in which separate 'fares' are paid by the various passengers, given certain conditions relating to advertising and to other factors which are designed to restrict the activity as a commercial, rather than social, activity. In similar vein, the drivers of 8 to 16-seat 'community buses' will be relieved of the need to obtain public service vehicle licences, so long as they are unpaid volunteers operating a service with essentially social or welfare objectives. But community bus services will continue to be restricted by the Traffic Commissioners in areas where they would compete with commercial services.

In two important respects, therefore, the Bill makes progress along lines suggested in this chapter — by strengthening the role of the county councils at the centre of the rural planning stage, and by redefining the sensitive interface between laissez-faire and the protection of existing operators. Many of the other ideas enunciated in this book remain to be formally incorporated into policy — in particular the clear shift that is needed towards explicit 'accessibility planning and management'. Three things will be needed if such an approach is to be widely adopted in the 1980s — sufficient money to ensure the provision of an otherwise unremunerative basic network of services, closer working and strengthened ties between the county councils and the other relevant agencies, and real political commitment. Many county councils may prove to be somewhat bashful about carrying out their now very clear responsibilities and in this case central government may have to move reluctantly but firmly into the area of defining precise levels of service which the councils must assure. For reasons already discussed this would be an unfortunate step, but only the 1980s will show whether it becomes necessary.

The above postscript was written just before the book went to press in July 1978. Since then, events have continued to move quickly — particularly as the Transport Bill is now law — and the task of proof-reading (November 1978) provides a chance to make some final observations.

There is now a real head of steam behind the rural deprivation 'backlash' to the apparently pro-urban emphasis of recent government policy. The Rural Community Councils[1] have produced the most comprehensive and damning indictment yet of the decline of rural services, and the associations of non-metropolitan county and district councils are becoming increasingly critical of 'big city bias' in rate support settlements. But Government awareness seems to be growing: the Department of Environment is about to launch four major research projects — on the social effects of rural primary school reorganization, decision-making by public authorities in rural areas, the nature of rural deprivation, and the concentration/dispersal dilemma in rural settlement planning. Given the time-lag between research and policy this suggests the possibility of major new departures in rural planning in the early 1980s.

But the 1970s are ending with a flurry, albeit a geographically patchy flurry, of new activity in the field of rural transport. The Parliamentary Select Committee on Nationalized Industries has completed an examination of the National Bus Company focusing very much on innovations in rural bus services.[2] Their report and its lengthy appendices constitute a good review of rural transport problems and policies in 1978.

The committee was evidently impressed by the scope for further community bus schemes and advocated their extension. With the lessons from the Rutex schemes (see p. 138) due soon, there will clearly be no shortage of advice for volunteers on how to complement the conventional provision of rural transport. The NBC's pamphlet 'With a little help from your friends' was produced in this vein, and the Department of Transport will shortly release a 'guide to community transport', interpreting for the layman some of the opportunities opened up by the recent legislation. And one district council at least, Breckland in Norfolk, has now established a 'voluntary Transport Schemes Fund' of £10,000 to foster social car schemes, car sharing and minibus and community bus services run by volunteers.

The other major relevant innovation of the 1978 Act, as explained above, concerns its attempt to promote a better

---

[1] Standing Conference of Rural Community Councils (1978) *The decline of rural services* (National Council of Social Service, London).

[2] House of Commons Select Committee on Nationalised Industries (1978) *Eighth Report: Innovations in Rural Bus Services*. HMSO.

transport planning process at the county level. In this context, NBC's Market Analysis Project (MAP) must be mentioned. MAP, which was born in the Midlands in 1977-8, is destined to become common practice throughout NBC's subsidiaries within three years. MAP is intended to uncover the best possible *commercially viable* network and fare-structure, by means both of rigorous appraisals of existing services and resources and of extensive on-bus and home interviews. It cannot replace the county councils' comprehensive transport planning function, being concerned only with scheduled and commercially viable NBC services. But it could provide a firm base-network upon which the counties might build the socially justified services they wish to commission.

The ball is now clearly and properly in the county councils' court. Much will depend on the degree of skill and enthusiasm with which they prepare and implement the new 'county public transport plans'. In this respect one is not encouraged by the recent observations made by the leader of one county council who sees the PTPs as 'a political public relations exercise and a waste of time and money' (*Kings Lynn News and Advertiser*, 24 October 1978). It is too soon to say whether such a view will be widely held, but it is certain that in the final analysis, the resolution of the rural accessibility problem will rest not on technical analyses but on political will.

Bibliography

Below are listed the references cited in the text. This listing does not pretend to be a comprehensive bibliography of rural transport and accessibility. For this, the reader is referred to Volume 2 of Moseley *et al.* (1977). Good starting points for further reading are provided by White (1976) on public transport and Cherry (1976) on rural planning problems. The reports by the Countryside Review Committee (1976, 1977) give an overview of rural Britain in the mid-1970s.

NOTE: The material referred to in the text as the UEA study is referenced as Moseley *et al.* 1977.

AGE CONCERN (1973), *On Transport*, National Old People's Welfare Council, London.

ASSOCIATION OF TRANSPORT COORDINATING OFFICERS (1976), *Findings of standards of service working party*, ATCO, Cheshire County Council.

BAINS REPORT (1972), *The new local authorities — management and structure*, H.M.S.O.

BEDFORDSHIRE COUNTY COUNCIL (1975), *Bedfordshire rural transport study: sector 1 north west*, County Council, Bedford.

BREHENY, M.J. (1974), 'Towards measures of spatial opportunity', *Progress in Planning*, 2.2 ed. D. Diamond and J.B. McLoughlin, Pergamon, Oxford.

BRIGGS, D.A. and JONES, P.M. (1973), 'Problems in transportation planning for the conurbation: the role of accessibility', unpublished paper, Institute of British Geographers' Conference, Birmingham.

BRITISH ROAD FEDERATION (1977), *Transport policies and programmes 1978/79-1982/83*, B.R.F., London.

BROWN, M. and WINYARD, S. (1975), *Low pay on the farm*, Low Pay Unit, London.

BUTCHER, H., *et al.* (1976), *Information and action service for rural areas — a case study in West Cumbria*, York University Department of Social Administration and Social Work, Papers in Community Studies No. 4.

CAMBRIDGESHIRE AND ISLE OF ELY COUNTY COUNCIL (1968), *Development plan review 1968: report of survey*, County Council, Cambridge.

CARLSTEIN, T. (1975), *A time-geographic approach to time allocation and socio-ecological systems*, Department of Geography, University of Lund, Sweden.

CARPENTER, T.C. (1976), 'The Postbus in Scotland', *Transport and Road Research Laboratory Symposium on unconventional bus services*, TRRL, Crowthorne, Berkshire.

CHERRY, G.E. (ed.) (1976), *Rural planning problems*, Leonard Hill.

CLARK, C. (1966), Industrial location and economic potential, *Lloyds Bank Review*, October.

CLARK, D. and UNWIN, K.I. (1977), *Information needs and information provision in rural areas: a pilot study*, Department of Geography, Lanchester Polytechnic, Coventry.

CLOKE, P.J. (1977), 'An index of rurality for England and Wales', *Regional Studies* 11. 31-46.

CLOUT, H.D., *et al.* (1972), *A study of the provisioon of public transportation in North Norfolk*, Department of Geography, University College, London.

CULLINGWORTH, J.B. (1976), *Town and country planning in Britain*, Allen & Unwin, London.

CUMMING, C. (1971), *Studies in educational costs*, Scottish Academic Press, Edinburgh.

COUNTRYSIDE REVIEW COMMITTEE (1976), *The countryside — problems and policies: a discussion paper*, H.M.S.O.

COUNTRYSIDE REVIEW COMMITTEE (1977), *Rural communities: a discussion paper*, Topic Paper No. 1, H.M.S.O.

DALY, A. (1975), 'Measuring accessibility in a rural context', *Rural Transport Seminar 1975*, Ed. P.R. White, Transport Studies Group, Polytechnic of Central London.

DEARLOVE, J. (1973), *The politics of policy in local government*, Cambridge University Press.

DEPARTMENT OF ENVIRONMENT (1971a), *Study of rural transport in Devon, report of the steering group*, London.

DEPARTMENT OF ENVIRONMENT (1971b), *Study of rural transport in West Suffolk, report of the steering group*, London.

DEPARTMENT OF ENVIRONMENT (1976), *Transport policy: a consultation document*, H.M.S.O.

DEPARTMENT OF ENVIRONMENT (1977), *Policy for the inner cities*, Cmnd 6845, H.M.S.O.

DEPARTMENT OF HEALTH AND SOCIAL SECURITY (1974), *Guidance memorandum on community hospitals: their role and development in the National Health Service*, HSC (IS) 75, DHSS, London.

DEPARTMENT OF TRANSPORT (1977), *Transport policy*, Cmnd 6836, H.M.S.O.

DEPARTMENT OF TRANSPORT (1978a), *Transport statistics, Great Britain 1966-76*, H.M.S.O.

DEPARTMENT OF TRANSPORT (1978b), *Transport Supplementary Grant submissions for 1979/80*, Circular 3/78, Dept. of Transport, London.

DERBYSHIRE COUNTY COUNCIL (1975), *Rural public transport study: report*, County Council, Matlock.

DEVELOPMENT COMMISSION (1977), *Thirty-fifth report of the Development Commissioners for the year ended 31 March 1977*, H.M.S.O.

DODS, J. (1978), 'Lost opportunities: passenger vehicle licensing and the law', *Solving the transport problems of the elderly: the use of resources*, ed. J. Garden, Department of Adult Education, University of Keele.

EAST ANGLIA REGIONAL STRATEGY TEAM (1974), *Strategic choice for East Anglia*, H.M.S.O.

EDDISON, A. (1973), *Local government management and corporate planning*, Leonard Hill.

ENNOR, P.D. (1976), 'Public transport in rural areas: a review', *Transport and Road Research Laboratory Symposium on unconventional bus services*, TRRL, Crowthorne, Berkshire.

GARDEN, J. (ed.) (1978), *Solving the transport problems of the elderly: the use of resources*, Department of Adult Education, University of Keele.

GOULD, P. (1969), *Spatial diffusion*, Commission on College Geography, Association of American Geographers, Washington D.C.

GREEN, R.J. (1971), *Country planning: the future of rural regions*, Manchester University Press.

HAGERSTRAND, T. (1970) 'What about people in regional science?', *Papers regional science association*, 24, 7-21.

HAGERSTRAND, T. (1973), 'The domain of human geography', *New directions in geography*, ed. R.J. Chorley, Methuen, London.

HAGERSTRAND, T. (1974), 'Transport in the 1980-1990 decade — the impact of transport on the quality of life', paper presented at the Fifth International Symposium on the Theory and Practice of Transport Economics at Athens, October 1973.

HALL, P. (1975), *Urban and regional planning*, Penguin, Harmondsworth.

HANNAN, D.F. (1969), 'Migration motives and migration differentials among Irish rural youth', *Sociologia Ruralis*, 9, 195-220.

HAYNES, R.M. (1978), 'Community attitudes towards the accessibility of hospitals in West Norfolk', *Social issues in rural Norfolk*, ed. M.J. Moseley, Centre of East Anglian Studies, University of East Anglia, Norwich.

HELLING, R. (1976), 'Recent research at Polytechnic of Central London:

the effect of public transport service cuts', *Rural Transport Seminar, 1976*, ed. P.R. White, Transport Studies Group, Polytechnic of Central London.

HILL, M. (1968), 'A goals-achievement matrix for evaluating alternative plans', *Journal of American Institute of Planners*, 34, 19-29.

HILLMAN, M. *et al.* (1973), *Personal mobility and transport policy*, Political and Economic Planning, Broadsheet 542, London.

HILLMAN, M. *et al.* (1976), *Transport realities and planning policy*, Political and Economic Planning, Broadsheet 567, London.

H.M. TREASURY (1978), *The government's expenditure plans, 1978-79 to 1981-82*, Cmnd 7049, H.M.S.O.

INGRAM, D.R. (1971), 'The concept of accessibility: a search for an operational form', *Regional Studies*, 5(2), 101-7.

JACK COMMITTEE (1961), *Rural bus services: report of the committee*, Ministry of Transport, H.M.S.O., London.

JACKMAN, R. (1978), 'Assessing rates needs', *New Society*, January, 72.

JANSEN, C.J. (1968), *Social aspects of internal migration: a research report*, Bath University Press.

JANSEN, C.J. (1969), 'Some sociological aspects of migration', *Migration*, ed. J.A. Jackson, Cambridge University Press.

JOHNSTON, R.J. (1966), An index of accessibility and its use in the study of bus services and settlement patterns', *Tijdschrift voor Economische en Sociale Geografie*, 57, 33-8.

JONES, P.M. (1975), 'Accessibility, mobility and travel need: some problems of definition and measurement', *Transport Studies Unit (Oxford) Note*, No.4.

LARKIN, A. (1978), 'Housing deprivation', *Rural deprivation and planning*, ed. J.M. Shaw, Geo Books, Norwich.

LEA, W. and ARCHIBALD, N. (1976), *Passenger transport coordination:a shire county's approach*, Transportation Unit, Cheshire County Council.

LEE, T. (1957), 'On the relations between the school journey and social and emotional adjustment in rural infant children', *British Journal of Educational Psychology*, 27, 101-14.

LICHFIELD, N. *et al.* (1975), *Evaluation in the planning process*, Pergamon, Oxford.

McTAVISH, A.D. *et al.* (1978), 'Concessionary travel schemes for the elderly', *Solving the transport problems of the elderly: the use of resources*, ed. J. Garden, Department of Adult Education, University of Keele.

MARTENSSON, S. (1975), 'Time-use and social organisation', *Symposium on Quality of Life*, Department of Geography, University of Lund, Sweden.

MARTIN, I. (1976), 'Rural communities', *Rural planning problems*, ed. G.E. Cherry, Leonard Hill.

MITCHELL, C.B. (1976), 'Some social aspects of public passenger transport', *Transport and Road Research Laboratory Symposium on unconventional bus services*, TRRL, Crowthorne, Berkshire.

MITCHELL, C.G.B. and TOWN, S.W. (1976), *Accessibility of various social groups to different activities*, Transport and Road Research Laboratory, Crowthorne, Berkshire.

MOSELEY, M.J., HARMAN, R.G., COLES, O.B. and SPENCER, M.B. (1977), *Rural Transport and Accessibility*, final report to Department of Environment, Centre of East Anglian Studies, University of East Anglia, Norwich, 2 vols.

MOYES, A. (1975), 'Aspects of County Council attitudes to the Rural Bus Subsidy Problem', *Regional studies association conference on rural public transport and planning*, ed. P.H.M. Wilmers and M.J. Moseley, Discussion Paper 4, The Association, London.

NORFOLK COUNTY COUNCIL (1977), *Norfolk structure plan*, County Council, Norwich.

OFFICE OF POPULATION CENSUSES AND SURVEYS (1977), *Population projections 1975-2015*, OPCS Series, pp.2 No.7 H.M.S.O.

OWENS, S. (1978), 'Changing accessibility in two North Norfolk parishes, Trunch and Southrepps, from the 1950s to the 1970s', *Social issues in rural Norfolk*, ed. M.J. Moseley, Centre of East Anglian Studies, University of East Anglia, Norwich.

OXFORDSHIRE COUNTY COUNCIL (1976), *Local transport in Oxfordshire*, County Council, Oxford.

OXLEY, P.R. (1976), 'Dial-a-ride in the UK: a general study', *Transport and Road Research Laboratory Symposium on unconventional bus services*, TRRL, Crowthorne, Berkshire.

PLOWDEN, S.P.C. (1974), *The future of transportation studies*, Mimeo, Metra Consulting Group Ltd, London.

REES, G. and WRAGG, R. (1975), *A study of the passenger transport needs of rural Wales*, Welsh Council, Cardiff.

RHYS, D.G. and BUXTON, M.J. (1974), 'Car ownership and the rural transport problem', *Chartered Inst. of Transport Journal*, 36, 109-12.

ROGERS, A.W. (1976), 'Rural housing', *Rural planning problems*, ed. G.E. Cherry, Leonard Hill.

ROSE, D. (1978), 'The political basis of rural deprivation: a case study', *Rural deprivation and planning*, ed. J.M. Shaw, Geo Books, Norwich.

SHAW, J.M. (1976), 'Can we afford villages?' *Built environment*, June, 135-7.

SHERMAN, L. et al. (1974), *Methods of evaluating metropolitan accessibility*, Transportation Research Record 449, Washington D.C.

Social Trends (1976), H.M.S.O.

STOCKFORD, R.P.H. (1978), 'Social services provision in rural Norfolk', *Social issues in rural Norfolk*, ed. M.J. Moseley, Centre of East Anglian Studies, University of East Anglia, Norwich.

STOPHER, P.R. and MAYBURG, A.H. (1975), *Urban transportation modelling and planning*, Lexington.

TANNER, J.C. (1977), *Car ownership trends and forecasts*, TRRL Laboratory Report 799, Transport and Road Research Laboratory, Crowthorne, Berkshire.

TRENCH, S. (1975), 'Economic criteria and transport subsidies', *Regional Studies Association conference on rural public transport and planning*, ed. P.H.M. Wilmers and M.J. Moseley, Discussion Paper 4, The Association, London.

WACHS, M. and KUMAGAI, T.C. (1972), *Physical accessibility as a social indicator*, School of Architecture and Urban Planning, University of California.

WEDDERBURN, D. (ed.) (1974), *Poverty, inequality and class structure*, Cambridge University Press.

WHITE, P.R. (1974), The cost of retaining British rural stage mileage lost since 1960', *Rural transport seminar 1974*, ed. P.R. White, Transport Studies Group, Polytechnic of Central London.

WHITE, P.R. (ed.) (1975), *Rural transport seminar 1975*, Transport Studies Group, Polytechnic of Central London.

WHITE, P.R. (1976), *Planning for public transport*, Hutchinson, London.

WOODRUFFE, B.J. (1976), *Rural settlement policies and plans*, Oxford University Press.

Index